The New Testament texts were produced with a high level of literary artistry, so it only makes sense that we use the arts to better understand them. This creative book is a wonderful visual exploration of the design and main themes of every New Testament book. Highly recommended!

TIM MACKIE
Cofounder of BibleProject

Patrick Schreiner has undertaken to give us something desperately needed among modern-day Bible readers: context. And he has done so in a way that is accessible and memorable. Useful for both those wanting to teach and those wanting to learn, here is a tool for grasping the "big picture" of each New Testament book using, of all things, pictures. May it aid many in having not just ears to hear the Word in context, but also eyes to see.

JEN WILKIN
Author and Bible teacher

I've always wished I had a brilliant Bible tutor sitting beside me when I study God's Word. It's so easy to misunderstand the layers of truth because of confusion around connecting themes, people, and understanding crucial verses. Now, with Patrick Schreiner's new book, *The Visual Word*, we finally have that! It's a one-stop shop that outlines the New Testament books with brilliant visual illustrations and imagery that gets us into the main storyline of the Scriptures in a fresh way. Any time you read the New Testament, this is the book you should keep right next to your Bible to serve as a guide as you work through God's Word.

LYSA TERKEURST
#1 *New York Times* bestselling author and president of Proverbs 31 Ministries

As continual learners of the Scripture and teachers as well, this resource will be much used in our home. To see the Word of God come to life through illustrations helps us not only remember them but also teach them better. We believe that seeing the whole of the book is a game-changer in understanding the message, and this book helps the reader see the context and message in a clear way. We are so grateful for this resource in our personal studies!

AARON AND JAMIE IVEY
Pastor at The Austin Stone Community Church; host of *The Happy Hour with Jamie Ivey* podcast; authors of *Complement: The Surprising Beauty of Choosing Together Over Separate in Marriage*

As a plane ride above the horizon helps you appreciate the place you call home, some books help you appreciate the big picture of God's wisdom in Scripture. *The Visual Word* is one of those books. This fascinating work stirs the reader with wonder in God's Word in a fresh way by combining succinct summaries and striking graphics that are not only creative but clear, faithful, memorable, and Christ-exalting. I highly commend it.

J. GARRETT KELL
Pastor, Del Ray Baptist Church, Alexandria, VA; author of *Pure in Heart: Sexual Sin and the Promises of God*

When we're serious enough about the Bible to want to grasp the argument or storyline of a book, many of us need help to organize our thoughts. *The Visual Word* provides us with fabulous one-page diagrams that imprint the original author's organization and emphasis in our minds, leading us to greater understanding and more faithful interpretation and application.

NANCY GUTHRIE
Author and Bible teacher

I have never seen a book that allows one to see the outline/summary of each New Testament book with such clarity and artistic beauty as I find in *The Visual Word*. It's accessible and attractive enough for kids and students to read, but thorough enough for seminarians and pastors to use as well. I absolutely love the visual format and the short summaries that supplement the various artistic icons. Whether you are exploring the Christian faith, are new to the Christian faith, or are leading others into deeper understanding of the New Testament, I would encourage you to grab this resource, grab a Bible, and journey along with Schreiner and Benedetto. I will be recommending it to many others.

TONY MERIDA
Pastor for Preaching, Imago Dei Church, Raleigh, NC; dean of Grimké Seminary

To combat biblical illiteracy we need resources to help readers better understand Scripture, but we also need resources that help readers *love* Scripture. *The Visual Word* is a resource that does both. Combining concise written summaries with beautiful illustrations, this book teaches the New Testament in a way that engages our mind and our heart. Truly unique and creatively presented, this is an exciting new tool to add to your Bible study toolbox.

BRETT MCCRACKEN
Senior editor at The Gospel Coalition; author of *The Wisdom Pyramid: Feeding Your Soul in a Post-Truth World* and *Uncomfortable: The Awkward and Essential Challenge of Christian Community*

A good roadmap by a trustworthy guide is one of the best tools in navigating your way through unfamiliar or difficult terrain. That's not only true when it comes to visiting a physical place but also in studying literary and historical texts like the New Testament. In these brilliant pages, New Testament scholar Patrick Schreiner teams up with the gifted theological artist Anthony Benedetto to summarize every section of the New Testament, with each one complemented by an illustration that helps us see and remember the message at a glance. I love creative resources like this. I expect to use it for years to come. And I pray it is used far and wide to instruct and encourage the church today.

JUSTIN TAYLOR
Managing editor of the ESV Study Bible

The Visual Word is one of the most exciting projects I've come across in a long time! I found myself engrossed in the visual outlines and imagery, pulling out my Bible to follow along, to see the broad contours of the narratives and logical flow of the arguments. This will become an excellent aid to believers who want to better understand the New Testament.

TREVIN WAX
Senior vice president for Theology and Communications at Lifeway Christian Resources, general editor of The Gospel Project, and author of *Rethink Your Self: The Power of Looking Up Before Looking In* and *This Is Our Time: Everyday Myths in Light of the Gospel*

Over the years many within the church have shifted away from a beautiful and compelling aesthetic to a more functional, utilitarian expression of the faith, and the church is lesser because of it. Patrick Schreiner gives the church a gift in *The Visual Word* by demonstrating the beauty of Scripture, not just in word but in visual form. I hope you will get a copy of *The Visual Word* and I think the Lord will use it to remind you of His beauty and the beauty of His Word.

MICAH FRIES
Director of Engagement, GlocalNet; author of *Leveling the Church*

What we need more than ever right now in our culture is scholars doing the work of deep biblical study coupled with a pastor's heart and artistic excellence. Sadly that's a rare combo these days, but Patrick knocks it out of the park with this one. His level of scholarship plus creativity is so engaging and enrapturing, and I can't wait to buy ten of these to hand out to friends!

JEFFERSON BETHKE
New York Times bestselling author of *Take Back Your Family*

THE VISUAL WORD

ILLUSTRATED OUTLINES OF THE NEW TESTAMENT BOOKS

PATRICK SCHREINER

ILLUSTRATED BY ANTHONY M. BENEDETTO

MOODY PUBLISHERS

CHICAGO

© 2021 by
PATRICK SCHREINER

Edited by Connor Sterchi
Interior design: Erik M. Peterson
Cover and illustrations by: Anthony M. Benedetto

Library of Congress Cataloging-in-Publication Data

Names: Schreiner, Patrick, author. | Benedetto, Anthony M., 1982-
   illustrator.
Title: The visual word : illustrated outlines of the New Testament books /
   by Patrick Schreiner ; illustrated by Anthony Benedetto.
Description: Chicago : Moody Publishers, [2021] | Includes bibliographical
   references. | Summary: "The Bible can be confusing. Wouldn't it be great
   if someone who understands the whole New Testament would put it together
   in one place? In The Visual Word, biblical scholar Patrick Schreiner
   depicts the contours of the New Testament and its underlying structure
   in visual format along with clear explanations"-- Provided by publisher.
Identifiers: LCCN 2020057848 (print) | LCCN 2020057849 (ebook) | ISBN
   9780802419279 (paperback) | ISBN 9780802497925 (ebook)
Subjects: LCSH: Bible. New Testament--Outlines, syllabi, etc. | Bible. New
   Testament--Illustrations.
Classification: LCC BS2525 .S37 2021 (print) | LCC BS2525 (ebook) | DDC
   225.02/02--dc23
LC record available at https://lccn.loc.gov/2020057848
LC ebook record available at https://lccn.loc.gov/2020057849

Originally delivered by fleets of horse-drawn wagons, the affordable paperbacks from D. L. Moody's publishing house resourced the church and served everyday people. Now, after more than 125 years of publishing and ministry, Moody Publishers' mission remains the same—even if our delivery systems have changed a bit. For more information on other books (and resources) created from a biblical perspective, go to www.moodypublishers.com or write to:

Moody Publishers
820 N. LaSalle Boulevard
Chicago, IL 60610

1 3 5 7 9 10 8 6 4 2

Printed in the United States of America

Dedication (Patrick)
To the many pastors
who have helped me
along the way
(Mark 8:27; 10:17; Acts 24:14).

John Piper (MN), Kevin Hash (KY), Thomas Weakley (KY),
Mark Dever (DC), Ryan Fullerton (KY), Jared Pulliam (OR)

Dedication (Anthony)
To my family, the Cassidys, Benedettos,
Singletons, Urbanos, and Garcias.
And to my family in Christ: the church,
His beautiful bride.

Thank You (Patrick)
To Moody for believing in this project.
To Anthony for working through these outlines with me.
To MBTS, Dr. Allen and Dr. Duesing, for their support.
To the SBC for investing in the future of churches.
To Hannah for standing beside me.

Thank You (Anthony)
To Moody for their confidence and freedom.
To Patrick for his interest in my work and trust in me.
To Annie for her excitement and support.

CONTENTS

INTRODUCTION

WHAT IS THIS BOOK?

You probably don't have another book like this in your library.

This book is a visual representation of the literary structure of each New Testament book. It is meant to give you a quick overview of the author's argument and the flow of their work.

Here is a brief rundown of the design.

On the right page, at the beginning of each New Testament book, is the heart of this project: visual, literary outlines with the main theme identified at the top. We have created icons, titles, and descriptions to summarize major sections of each book and show how they relate to one another.

On the left page are short thematic and literary summaries of each book in paragraph form. This gives readers brief overviews in writing, supplementing the graphics on the right.

The subsequent pages have the icons of the respective literary sections with matching paragraphs further explaining the section. These summaries are not exhaustive. The point of them is to give a sense of the literary flow and main points if someone wants to read more about each section.

In terms of design, each visual element, including the layout, has been carefully thought through. For example, the Johannine literature has been displayed in circular form because John writes in a circular fashion. The background colors of the icon pages also match the different sections of Scripture.

CANONICAL LAYOUT	
THE GOSPELS	GOLD
ACTS & THE GENERAL EPISTLES	GRAY
PAULINE LITERATURE	DARK BLUE
REVELATION	GOLD

The only book that doesn't fit the typical early church division is Hebrews, which was usually associated with Pauline literature; however we made it gray as it seems unlikely Paul wrote it. Given that more textual traditions link Acts with the General Epistles, Acts has a gray background.

Readers will notice we have usually kept verse references out of the main headings. This was done for the sake of clarity. I wanted to give people a quick overview without tripping over verse references. Readers can identify more specific verse divisions in the subsections.

WHY I WROTE THIS BOOK

I wrote this book for three reasons. First, I believe one of the most important things to do when reading the Bible is to *read it contextually.* For most, this means historical context. This is vitally important, but this book focuses on the literary context. The Bible contains verses, but these verses come in chapters, books, and a larger storyline. Many people have a favorite verse but can't tell where it sits in the flow of the author's idea or even in the placement of the story. To read well, readers must follow the flow of an author's argument.

Each book of the Bible contains a story. An argument. Like a symphony or a play, the Bible was not put together haphazardly but carefully designed to communicate something. In a time where attention spans are becoming shorter and entertainment increasingly more available, it is difficult to sustain concentration through the Bible. This book is meant to help by giving a visual overview of the structure of each book of the New Testament. This leads me to my next point.

Second, *I learn visually.* Though the Bible is not written visually, I believe we are free to use aids to help us learn the Bible more thoroughly. I find that I can grasp things and remember them better if I can see them. If they are arranged spatially. Students have had similar experiences in my classes. As I began drawing forms of these designs up on the whiteboard as I taught, I could see things clicking in the students' minds as we followed the author's train of thought.

Though I wrote the book, Anthony Benedetto did all the illustrations. We talked over each image and the outline of each book in great detail. So it would be worthwhile to pay attention. Easter eggs shall be found. Even the details are important. He did an amazing job, and much of this book is due to his diligent work.

Third, I wrote this book because *I have a bad memory.* I am an instructor who teaches overview classes on the Bible. It is hard for me to remember the flow of a book with all the information I want to get across. To help me remember at a quick glance what is happening, I began drawing out visual outlines of books in a Moleskine, taking some cues from Tim Mackie at the BibleProject. I found it jogged my memory more quickly than a compendium of notes that have no visual appeal or layout.

HOW TO USE THIS BOOK

For most of you this is not a typical book on the Bible, so how should you use it?

For **church members and attenders**, this book can be used as you go through your own Bible reading plan to get a better grasp on the literary overview of the different books. I would recommend giving the chart a glance before you start reading. Then after you have finished reading each section, look back at the icon that summarizes it and read the corresponding paragraph. Then when you finish, give the overview another glance and see if it begins to click.

For **pastors**, this book can be a good first step to get an overview of a book for a sermon series. I have found commentaries rarely helpful in this regard. The long detailed outlines at the beginning of these books do little for preachers. Even if you don't agree with everything I have put here or want to phrase things differently, these can begin stirring your imagination and give you a good sense of the larger sections and how they cohere. The visual outlines could be displayed during the series to give the congregation a visual overview as well.

For **Sunday School teachers**, **lay Bible instructors**, **parents**, and **professors (graduate or undergraduate)**, this book can be used when you teach overviews of each New Testament book. It can be a supplemental or core resource that you require of your listeners. I would recommend displaying the outlines to your audience on a screen as you go through each book so they too can see a visual representation of the literary structure.

For **students**, this book can be used as a textbook or supplemental text to help you remember the literary structure of different New Testament books. I have found that most outlines in commentaries are too long, and most introductory textbooks are too short. I hope these outlines hit that middle ground, and the visual aids help people grasp the beauty and the depth of the Scriptures.

THREE CAVEATS

Three caveats or warnings are worth mentioning before you begin.

First, I don't believe there is "one" literary structure for each book, though I do believe there are better and worse structures. Many good outlines show different things. Outlines are like constellations. Clues (stars) in the text exist, but the reader is drawing lines between the stars to make sense of them. Some lines are clearer than others.

Second, though this may be obvious, it is worth mentioning we were constrained in our designs by the page size and the number of circles we could fit on a page. We wanted to make the outlines visually appealing and minimalistic as much as possible. However, in so doing, that means that sometimes we had to sacrifice ideas for design.

Third, I present these outlines as an initial proposal. When Drew Dyck approached me and asked if I wanted to turn the visual outlines I had posted on Twitter into a book, I first said I think it would be better if I waited ten to twenty years. I said this because I know as I study more, teach more, and think more I will gain greater clarity and things might shift. He rightly responded with two considerations. There is no guarantee I will have those years, and we can always do a second or third edition. Touché Drew.

If you find this helpful, feel free to share this book with your friends. If this one is a success, we hope to do the Old Testament as well. If it is not a success, then all you get is the New Testament. The choice is yours!

Happy reading and seeing.

A WORD FROM THE ILLUSTRATOR (ANTHONY)

The magnitude of this project was daunting on many levels. First was the weight of seeking to interpret the Word of God visually, and second was the sheer amount of imagery required to illuminate each book in the New Testament. Twenty-five outlines with approximately twelve custom icons per outline—I'll let you do the math. Though it was incredibly challenging, the project came at a time of need and has served to be a tremendous blessing throughout. It was a joy to get to know Patrick during the process, and we had many meaningful conversations, and laughs, along the way.

My hope is that the illustrated iconography will do two things. First, that it would help add a bit of creative, even narrative, content to Patrick's words. Second, that the visual images would become anchors for the reader to remember and recall the information they've learned. Ultimately, I hope that the beauty of the book creates an enjoyable experience that draws readers back again and again.

I have always been fascinated by the closing of John's gospel. "This is the disciple who is bearing witness about these things, and who has written these things, and we know that his testimony is true. Now there are also many other things that Jesus did. Were every one of them to be written, I suppose that the world itself could not contain the books that would be written" (John 21:24–25).

I love God's Word, and as I walk with Christ, I am slowly seeing how truly expansive it is. It has been the highest privilege and blessing to seek to illuminate, in some small way, this most beautiful and terrifying mystery.

I hope and pray that God will use it to reveal, root, and build His church until He comes again!

MATTHEW

FULFILLMENT

Matthew is the doorway
of the New Testament.

A disciple of Jesus scripts the story of Jesus in the shape of the Old Testament. He teaches readers how the new fulfills the old. Jesus completes, fills up, and satisfies the story that began in Genesis. Matthew sets his eyes on Jesus, training future generations to walk in the footsteps of their Rabbi. Jesus is the Messiah, the new Abraham (who has many children from the East and West), the new David (who is the true king), the new Solomon (who is wise), the new Moses (who delivers the Torah), and the new Jeremiah (who laments the fate of Jerusalem).

The early church associated Matthew with a human face because of the theme of revelation. His outline closely tracks with the Old Testament story. He begins with a genealogy (1:1–17), echoing Genesis, and ends with a commission from Jesus (28:18–20) that mirrors Cyrus's at the end of 2 Chronicles. In the center are Jesus' parables about the mystery of the kingdom (13), causing readers to recall the wisdom tradition. The rest of the narrative fills out Israel's history. Jesus is supernaturally born, saved from a tyrant king, comes out of Egypt, goes through the water, into the wilderness, up the mountain, heals, sends out His disciples, and prophetically pronounces both judgment and hope upon those who listen. Ultimately, Jesus undergoes exile in His death. However, He is raised to life because of His innocent blood. He is the Mosaic-Davidic King.

MATTHEW / FULFILLMENT

WHO IS JESUS? 1

He is the son of David, the son of Abraham, and the Son of God.

WHERE IS HE FROM? 2

Jesus is from Bethlehem, Egypt, and Nazareth.

Preparation 3–4

Jesus is baptized by John and tempted.

Healings 8–9

The kingdom spreads; Jesus calls followers.

Rejection 11–12

Jesus is rejected, and reveals His true family.

Revelation 14–17

Jesus is transfigured before the disciples.

Reproof 21–22

Jesus enters Jerusalem and condemns it.

Wholeness 5–7

Flourishing comes by listening to Christ.

Witness 10

Jesus sends the disciples to proclaim the kingdom.

Mystery 13

Teaching on the mystery of the kingdom of God.

Household 18–20

Jesus' instructions and ethics for the church.

Judgment 23–25

Jesus gives the verdict on Israel's leaders.

CRUCIFIXION 26–27

Jesus submits to a kingly trial and death.

RESURRECTION 28

The victory of life, Jesus' commission and promise.

WHO IS JESUS? (1)

A list of names. It's an odd way to begin. But the genealogy shows readers this isn't a fairy tale, but a true story. Matthew opens with his convictions fully exposed. Jesus is the Christ, the son of David, the son of Abraham (1:1). The genealogy gives a Davidic family tree that proves Jesus is the new King of Israel. Not only that, but genealogies function prominently in the Old Testament with the promise of a seed (Gen. 3:15). Surprisingly, some in Jesus' family are Gentile women with checkered sexual pasts. They are all characterized by tenacious fidelity to Yahweh. However, Matthew's genealogy isn't primarily about people, but about a child and God Himself. God carries along this family line despite their failures (1:1–17). If the genealogy shows Jesus is the son of David and Abraham, then the birth narrative displays Jesus as the Son of God and son of Joseph (1:18–25). Jesus is conceived by the Holy Spirit. Joseph names Him according to the angel's command, thereby adopting Him. Joseph and Mary's situation resembles and fulfills Abraham's and Sarah's: both have supernatural births. Matthew 1 fulfills Genesis: a new creation, a new humanity, has arrived.

WHERE IS HE FROM? (2)

Some may have had questions about Jesus' origins. Matthew proves that all the places Jesus hails from fulfill Old Testament texts. He is their predicted Messiah. First, Jesus is from Bethlehem, the city of David (2:1–12). But another king already resides in Bethlehem, so Jesus and His family must flee. Herod is a tyrant (like Pharaoh) who acts violently against his people. Mary's child will be a Shepherd-King leading His people to quiet waters. Second, Jesus is from Egypt (2:13–15). Like Israel, Jesus must flee into Egypt for safety, but He and His people will come out of exile. This point is further reinforced by a reference to Ramah (2:16–18). Ramah was the place Israel departed for exile (Jer. 40:1), and now Rachel weeps for her children who are killed by Herod, but the hope of Jeremiah 31 is that the children shall come back to their own country. Finally, Jesus is from Nazareth. Nazareth derives from the word branch in Hebrew, and therefore fulfills the promise of a Davidic Branch (Isa. 11:1; Jer. 23:5; 33:15; Zech. 3:8). All of these places prove Jesus is their long-awaited Shepherd-King.

Preparation (3–4) / The Old Testament shadow stories continue. Jesus goes through water (3), into the wilderness (4), and then up the mountain (5–7). The first narrative puts John the Baptist in the shadow of Jesus with new exodus themes. John is the voice preparing the way for Jesus to bring His people out of exile (3:3). Jesus is baptized by John and anointed as the Messiah (3:13–17). Then Jesus is led into the wilderness to be tempted like Israel and Adam by Satan (4:1–11). But unlike Israel and Adam, He does not fail. He fully trusts God's Word, even when He is brought up to a high mountain and told He can be King without suffering. Jesus withdraws into Galilee because of John's death and begins His ministry centered on the announcement of the kingdom of heaven (4:12–22). He will not return to Jerusalem until His death.

Wholeness (5–7) / The Sermon on the Mount is one of the most famous passages in the Scriptures. In it, Jesus acts as the new Moses, mediating the new Torah. The sermon concerns what it means to flourish, to be whole, to be blessed in God's creation. Jesus argues this comes by having an all-encompassing righteousness: both inward and outward. The Torah was always meant to regulate human hearts, but it could not because of their sin and the lack of the Spirit. Jesus begins with words of comfort for those in exile (5:1–12). He offers them the upside-down kingdom. Then He gives them His thesis: He came to fulfill the Torah, teaching them about greater righteousness (5:17–20). This means they need to follow the true intention of the Torah (5:17–48), continue in giving to the poor, praying, and fasting (6:1–18), and finally, perform justice (6:19–7:12). Ultimately, they must love God and others (see 7:12). Jesus closes with a warning: they can take two paths, follow two prophets, and build on two different foundations (7:13–29). One path means life, the other death. One foundation means destruction, the other wholeness.

Healings (8–9) / Jesus has spoken of the kingdom; now He enacts the kingdom through His deeds. Ultimately, this paints Him as the Suffering Servant who gives His life for others. He welcomes the least likely into the kingdom. He brings the new creation by the touch of His hand. Nine miracles occur, many of them matching and reversing failures of the wilderness generation. First, Jesus comes to the marginalized: a man with leprosy, a centurion's servant, and Peter's mother-in-law (8:1–17). Then He calls others to follow Him, but many of them view it as too costly (8:18–22). Three more miracles occur: Jesus stills the storm, casts out demons, and heals a paralytic, forgiving his sins (8:23–9:8). Again, the narrative pauses as Jesus calls Matthew to come and follow Him, contrasting Matthew's response with those who refused earlier (9:9–17). Three final healings occur: Jesus heals the ruler's daughter and the sick woman, two blind men, and another demon-possessed man (9:18–34). The harvest is ripe, but more workers are needed (9:37).

Witness (10) / Matthew 1–9 has the shape of the Pentateuch. Chapter 10 begins with the conquest and entry into the land as Jesus sends out His disciples. The picture presented is one of taking territory for the kingdom of heaven, similar to the conquest of Canaan. After Jesus identifies the messengers (10:1–4), He tells them of their message, mission, and tools (10:5–10). They are to go into the land, let their peace fall on houses that welcome them, but judgment upon those that don't (10:11–15). When they enter the land, they will face persecution (10:16–42). They will be delivered over to courts, but they should not be anxious. There will be family division, but they are to endure to the end. They will be maligned, but they are to have no fear. Ultimately, if they acknowledge Jesus, He will acknowledge them. If they lose their life, they will find it.

Rejection (11–12) / If chapter 10 mirrored Israel's conquest, then Matthew 11–12 is about the monarchy and the various response to the new King. Jesus is questioned and rejected, but He defines His true family. Jesus continues to be presented as the new David. He is also the new Solomon. Three panels make up these chapters. First, Jesus is questioned on various issues: Is He the one they should be expecting (11:3), why do His disciples do what is not lawful on the Sabbath (12:2), and can this be the Son of David (12:23)? Jesus responds saying He is their redemption (11:5–6), He is like David but greater, and a kingdom divided against itself cannot stand (12:25–37). Then He condemns this generation for their unresponsiveness (11:16–24; 12:38–45). Ultimately, He says the kingdom is for little children (11:25), Gentiles (12:15–21), and those who do His will (12:46–50). His true family is being formed. Some are stumbling on the rock; others are built upon it.

Mystery (13) / The third discourse contains parables on the mystery of the kingdom. It parallels the wisdom tradition. Jesus describes the mystery of the kingdom and speaks in poetic form like David (Psalms) and his son Solomon (Proverbs). Matthew explicitly quotes from the Wisdom Literature, saying that these words fulfill the saying, "I will open my mouth in parables; I will utter what has been hidden since the foundation of the world" (Matt. 13:35; see Ps. 78:2). Jesus speaks about the *responses* to the kingdom message (13:1–23), the *growth* of the kingdom (13:24–43), and finally the *value* of the kingdom (13:44–52). He compares the kingdom to soil, a tree, a treasure, a pearl, and a net. Though His hearers might think they understand the kingdom plan, Jesus says it will grow slowly, be a mixed community, but is worth a greater price than anything this world has to offer. The mystery of the kingdom is that it is like a seed planted in the ground that looks unimpressive today. One day it will be a towering tree. The nations will find shade under it.

Revelation (14–17) / In chapters 14–17, Jesus reveals who He is through both Peter's confession and the transfiguration. But responses to Jesus also take center stage as Matthew moves out of the monarchy and wisdom tradition to the divided kingdom. Echoes of Elijah and Elisha fill out the narrative as Jesus continues to fulfill the Old Testament. Though Jesus is rejected in His hometown of Nazareth, He feeds the Jews as a greater prophet than Moses (13:53–14:36). Jesus clarifies defilement comes from the inside, not the outside (15:1–20). A more positive response is given by Gentiles, particularly a Canaanite woman, and Jesus feeds the Gentiles as well (15:21–39). The varying responses to Jesus come to a head when they ask Him for a sign, but He rebukes them for the question (16:1–12). This leads to Jesus revealing who He truly is to Peter, but even the disciples misunderstand His mission (16:13–27). Jesus shows them His glory on the mountain in the transfiguration as Moses and Elijah appear next to Him, but as they come off the mountain, the disciples still don't understand the only way to glory is through suffering (17:9–23).

Household (18–20) / The fourth discourse continues the prophetic theme and centers on the remnant, the new people of God. Through Jesus' visionary words, He establishes, teaches, and instructs His church. The new community even has its own structures of authority and the presence of God to enforce standards. The text is a household code for Jesus' new community, where He teaches them to be peaceable, forgive, and care for one another. In chapter 18, He tells them to reflect on their identity. They are to become like children in humility (18:1–6) and care for little ones (18:10–14). Likewise, they are instructed to be peacemakers (18:15–35) and care for one another, seeking out reconciliation. In chapter 19 they are instructed on domestic ethics: divorce (19:3–12), children (19:13–15), and wealth (19:16–30). Finally, chapter 20 sums up their vocation as His body. They are to be the last rather than first (20:1–16) and become servants to all (20:17–34). The remnant will be God's new community, His new household.

Reproof (21–22) / Matthew 21 marks a definite shift. Though Jesus has given hope to His remnant, from here onward Jesus is the "judging prophet." He enters the city of Jerusalem on a colt. Rather than coming into the city as the conquering and victorious Messiah, Jesus acts as the condemning prophet. Three related symbolic temple acts exemplify this (21). First, He confronts the temple system. Second, He castigates the leaders of Israel. Third, He foretells the temple's destruction. For Israel, the destruction of the temple and exile went hand in hand. Jesus is the new prophet denouncing the nation for their sins. The chapter ends with questions about where Jesus gets His authority (21:23–27), but He won't answer them. Then Jesus tells three parables about people not being obedient or ready for His return (21:28–22:14). The religious leaders question Him on three hot topics, trying to trap Him: politics, eschatology, and the interpretation of the Old Testament (22:15–40). Jesus halts the conversation by asking them a question they cannot answer (22:41–46). His wisdom and inspiration are unmatched. He is God's prophet.

Judgment (23–25) / In the final discourse, Jesus condemns the religious leaders as the rebuking prophet. This matches the censure by Jeremiah, Ezekiel, and Isaiah. He looks at Israel's leaders and pronounces judgment upon them using seven woes to condemn them, providing a contrast to the Beatitudes (23:1–36). Then Jesus laments the fate of Jerusalem (23:37–39). Matthew 24–25 describes both the end of the temple period and the end of the world in apocalyptic terms—exile is coming. The discourse begins with Jesus looking at the temple and predicting its destruction (24:1–2). The glory of the Lord is leaving the temple, as Ezekiel prophesied. For Jesus, the glory of the Lord is not only leaving the temple; the temple must also be destroyed. The last day is coming and no one knows the hour, but they all must be ready for the return of the King (24:36–25:30). When He returns, He will be a judging Shepherd, separating the sheep from the goats (25:31–46). Jesus has condemned the current generation. Now He will go and die for them.

CRUCIFIXION (26–27)

If Matthew is following the history of the Old Testament, the next thing that should happen is the destruction of the temple and the exile. Blood should fill this section as the people of Israel are attacked and destroyed by their enemies. The blood of Israel *is* spilled, but it is innocent blood. Jesus' blood. Blood turns out to be not only the cue to the exile and destruction of the temple but also the prompt for the rebuilding of the temple and the return from exile. Blood is both the curse and the cure. It lies at the center of Israel's future. First, Jesus prepares for His death under the banner of the Passover (26:1–46), then He is arrested and goes through trials (26:47–27:26), and finally He is crucified (27:27–66). His crucifixion is painted in royal hues as He is enthroned upon the hill of the skull. The King has been crowned. Hope comes in the most unexpected way.

RESURRECTION (28)

Death cannot stop innocent blood. Jesus conquers death by life. Jesus ends the exile through abundant life. Women come to visit the tomb of Jesus, but He is not there. Jesus meets them and tells them they have no reason to fear, while at the same time the chief priests craft a false tale about the disciples stealing Jesus' body (28:1–15). Then Jesus goes to a mountain in Galilee with the disciples. He gives them the command to make disciples of all nations because He has been given all authority as the Son of Man (28:16–20). He is not only the King of the Jews but the one presented before the Ancient of Days. Jesus promises His presence will be with them forever. Chronicles, the last book of the Hebrew Old Testament, also ends with a note about the restoration to come (2 Chron. 36:22–23). Cyrus gives a commission for Israel to go up to Jerusalem to rebuild the temple. Now the disciples are the temple-builders. They go out with the message and healing of King Jesus. His birth, life, death, and resurrection has fulfilled all that was predicted in the Old Testament.

MARK

THE SERVANT-KING

Mark's account is gritty
and unrelenting.

He takes readers on a discipleship journey as they witness the roar of the King, who unexpect-edly conquers by donning the crown of thorns. As Jesus reveals His identity, misunderstanding and conflict arise. The kingdom of God has arrived in this Servant, but many are not ready. A new gospel has erupted in the den of another kingdom. There will be a battle. Jesus defeats the empire's gospel and Satan's power with the strength of a lion, but the sacrifice of a lamb.

The early church associated Mark with a lion—one with all authority and power, who bounds about establishing the kingdom. Mark is structured around two questions: Who is Jesus (1–8:21), and how will He become king (11–16)? Between these two panels Jesus reveals along the way He is the Lion of the tribe of Judah who becomes King by suffering (8:22–10:52). Jesus' power is on full display as He exorcises, heals, forms a new community, and teaches. But this also causes conflict. Jesus discloses His true nature to His disciples: He is the Messiah, the Son of God, the son of David, the Son of Man. But they still misunderstand that His power and suffering are paired. To become King, He must bear the cross.

MARK / THE SERVANT-KING

JESUS' POWER   1-8

The rule of God causes conflict with Satan, nature, and Israel's leaders.

JESUS' SUFFERING   11-16

Jesus becomes the royal king by suffering and death.

Preparation   1:1-13

Jesus, the new exodus way, goes through water and conquers.

THE WAY   8-10

Jesus reveals who He is and how He will suffer to become king.

The Royal Entry   11-13

He enters the city as king and condemns the Jerusalem leaders.

Kingdom Arrival   1:14–8:21

Jesus' authority in providing food, healing, exorcising, and teaching.

Revelation   8:22-10:52

Peter confesses Jesus as Messiah and Jesus is transfigured.

Last Supper & Trial   14

His death is a new Passover meal; Jesus goes to trial.

Kingdom Community 1:14–8:21

Jesus calls, appoints, and sends His disciples out with His own authority.

Discipleship   8:22-10:52

The disciples misunderstand. Jesus' cross means their cross.

Jesus' Death   15

Jesus dies alone. A centurion recognizes He is the Son of God.

Kingdom Responses 1:14–8:21

The crowd, leaders, and even the disciples question Jesus' authority.

Jesus' Life   16

Jesus' tomb is empty. The women run in fear and confusion.

JESUS' POWER (1–8)

The lion roars as Jesus displays His power bounding from place to place. But He also silences people telling them to not publicize who He is yet. People are not ready for revolution. Jesus' power confronts cosmic and social orders as He exorcises, heals, and subdues nature. He also challenges Jewish practices, reframing their true intention. He forgives sins, works on the Sabbath, and redefines purity. He teaches, not as their scribes, but as one with authority. The responses to Jesus are largely negative. People question Him: Who can forgive sins but God? Why does He eat with sinners? Why is He doing what is not lawful? The religious leaders plot about how they can tame Him. But in the midst of opposition, He forms His own pride. He calls His disciples and sends them to proclaim and enact the kingdom.

Preparation (1:1–13) / Like Genesis, Mark opens with "beginning." However, unlike the gospels of Matthew and Luke, there is no birth narrative, no genealogy, no wise men, no shepherds. Though Mark will take his readers on a journey through the eyes of the disciples, his introduction is uncompromising and direct: Jesus is the new creation, the Messiah, the Son of God. Mark immediately conveys to readers into three important events that reveal Jesus' mission and identity: John the Baptist is identified as Jesus' forerunner (1:2–8), Jesus is baptized (1:9–11), and cosmic conflict with Satan occurs in the wilderness (1:12–13). Jesus' ministry is put in the shadow of return from exile themes. This theme of "the way" will return in 8:22–10:45. When Jesus is baptized by John, He is declared to be God's beloved Son. Two other Sonship revelation stories are located strategically at the transfiguration and cross (9:1–13; 15:21–41). Jesus' combat with Satan sets up the entire narrative as cosmic conflict. It gives hope to Roman martyrs who also encounter wild beasts.

Kingdom Arrival (1:14–8:21) / Who is Jesus? Mark has already let readers know through his introduction, but now he will press this point home by Jesus' words and actions. The kingdom arrives in King Jesus. As His ministry begins, Jesus gives a press conference of His gospel: the kingdom of God is at hand—repent and believe (1:14–15). This challenges the rule of Rome and the kingdom of Satan. The first display of authority comes in driving out a demon: the kingdom of God wars against the kingdom of darkness (1:21–28). The presence of the kingdom is further demonstrated in healings (1:29–34; 5:21–42; 6:53–56; 7:31–37), cleansing (1:39–45), forgiving sins (2:1–12), declaring Jesus is the Lord of the Sabbath (2:23–3:6), binding Satan (3:22–30), feeding (6:30–44; 8:1–10), subduing nature (4:35–41; 6:45–52), and driving out demons (5:1–18). And yet, it is not only His actions, but actions paired with preaching. Jesus states that He came to proclaim a message. His deeds fall under the banner of proclamation of a new kingdom

(1:35–38). The preaching and teaching receive the most attention in chapter 4 when He tells parables of the kingdom. These parables both reveal and conceal. The mystery of the kingdom's arrival is on full display.

Kingdom Community (1:14–8:21) / In the midst of the kingdom arrival, Jesus also forms a new kingdom community. A king calls subjects to follow him both in conquest and in the proliferation of peace. After Jesus has given His message in summary form (1:14–15), the first thing He does is call His first disciples and appoints them as fishers of men (1:16–20). They will join Him in the task of gathering others to this new society. Peppered throughout Jesus' teaching and healing are further calls: He commands Levi to follow Him (2:13–17), and then appoints the twelve apostles to preach and cast out demons with all authority (3:13–19; 6:7–13). A new army of goodness and harmony forms around the King. He also redefines His family as those who do His will (3:31–35). Neither blood nor ethnic ties give one a VIP pass into His family. Loyalty to the King is all that is required.

Kingdom Responses (1:14–8:21) / Though Jesus has demonstrated His power and authority, people respond with perplexity and negativity. Those who oppose Jesus question Him, the demons shudder at His presence, and even the disciples wonder at Him. When Jesus teaches, the crowd asks, "What is this? A new teaching with authority!" (1:27). The scribes query, "Who can forgive sins but God alone?" and "Why does he eat with tax collectors and sinners?" (2:7, 16). The Pharisees question why the disciples don't follow the Jewish traditions (2:24; 7:5), and His hometown questions where Jesus got this wisdom (6:2). Even the disciples ask, "Who then is this, that even the wind and the sea obey him?" (4:41). There is general confusion concerning His authority and the arrival of the kingdom. After all that Jesus has done, this section appropriately ends with Jesus asking the question: "Do you not yet understand?" (8:21).

THE WAY (8–10)

So who is Jesus, and how will He become king? The central section of Mark (8:22–10:52) reveals who Jesus is and reframes how the kingdom will come. Jesus then calls His disciples to also take up the cross. Jesus' messianic vocation means glory, but only through suffering and death. He is the Servant-King. This is "the way," and Jesus explains it to them along the way (8:27; 9:33–34; 10:17, 32, 46, 52). The section is therefore about revelation, and appropriately begins with a two-stage healing involving a blind man (8:22–26) and ends with a blind man seeing fully (10:46–52). Likewise, the disciples will progressively see Jesus with more clarity. Peter confesses

Jesus is the Messiah and Jesus is transfigured before them. The Father again declares, "This is my beloved Son" (9:7), but the disciples again misunderstand.

Revelation (8:22–10:52) / On the way, Jesus reveals Himself. Peter confesses that Jesus is the Messiah (8:27–30). Jesus is also transfigured before His disciples, and Elijah and Moses appear with Him (9:2–13). The veil has been removed for the disciples to see. Readers have already witnessed a similar scene in the baptism. The disciples now hear the Father affirm, "This is my beloved Son" (9:7). This claim is supported by His authority over demons (9:14–29) and authoritative teachings on the Torah (10:1–29). Ultimately, Jesus reveals that His kingship comes by servanthood. "For even the Son of Man came not to be served but to serve, and to give his life as a ransom for many" (10:45). After each revelation story, Jesus pairs it with a prediction of His suffering, death, and resurrection (8:31–33; 9:30–32; 10:32–34). In Jerusalem, He will be given over to the Roman Empire, and His enemies will mock Him and kill Him. He will even be betrayed by His own people, but three days later He will rise again. He will again be transfigured. Travail is coming, but so is transformation.

Discipleship (8:22–10:52) / Jesus reveals Himself on the way, but this revelation relates not only to His glory and power, but His suffering, agony, and crucifixion. Therefore, after Jesus has revealed His glory, He also predicts His death three times (8:31; 9:31; 10:32–34). The disciple wondered who Jesus is, and now they misunderstand His messianic calling (8:32–34; 9:33–34; 10:35–41). Peter rebukes Jesus for speaking about His death, the disciples argue about who will be the greatest, and James and John ask if they might sit on His right and left in His glory. Therefore, Jesus corrects them; He gives them a lesson in servant leadership. They must deny themselves and take up their crosses (8:34–9:1), they must become servants of all (9:35–37), and they must not lord their authority over others but become slaves to all (10:42–45). Jesus is a Servant-King, calling others to emulation.

JESUS' SUFFERING (11–16)

How will Jesus become the messianic king? He has already told them it must be by suffering, death, and resurrection. Now in Mark 11–16 those predictions are fulfilled. If the first half of Mark is about Jesus' power, this half is about His power *through* suffering. The Lion submits to His own demise. Jesus first enters Jerusalem and confronts the leaders and their places of power (11–13). Then Jesus conducts His last supper with His disciples and goes to trial (14–15). Jesus' crucifixion reveals His identity as the King of the Jews who sacrifices Himself for the nation and the world. A centurion recognizes Him as the Son of God *in* His suffering (15:39). Finally, His body is missing from the tomb, just as He predicted (16). Readers have been at eye level with the disciples all along, and continue to watch in shock, shame, amazement, and even fear.

The Royal Entry (11–13) / Jesus' royal entry is all about the temple. He enters the city as a conquering but humble king (11:1–11) and condemns the corrupt temple (11:12–21). God has tended His vineyard, but when He comes, there is no produce to be seen. Therefore, judgment awaits. The religious leaders understand Jesus' subversive actions, so they test Him. Jesus has now performed His most "authoritative" action in the temple and they ask Him where He gets the authority to do this (11:27–33). He answers by giving a parable about the vineyard, but they continue to test Him: about politics, party disagreements, and the explanation of the Torah (12:1–34). Jesus shuts down the conversation by stumping them with the Scripture (12:35–37). Playtime is over. Therefore, He pronounces the destruction of the temple connecting it to the coming of the Son of Man (13). Their rule is finished. A new Shepherd-King has arrived. These temple actions will spur on His death.

Last Supper & Trial (14) / Jesus' last days are numbered. The chief priests and the scribes search for a time to kill Him. A woman appropriately anoints Him for burial (14:1–9). Then Jesus celebrates the Passover with His disciples. This meal reveals the significance of the Christ's death. He is their new Moses, leading them out of exile. He is their sacrificial lamb, whose blood covers them from death. He is their new covenant leader, who gives them access to the presence of God. Jesus will die all alone. Judas betrays Him, and so does Peter. In the garden, the disciples flee from Him (14:32–50). Jesus goes to trial. He faces the Sanhedrin (His own people) and the empire (Pilate). Surprisingly, Pilate wants to release Him, but His blood relatives want Him crucified. A violent rebel is released instead of the Prince of Peace.

Jesus' Death (15) / Jesus' passion is depicted as a Roman triumph. In the first century, parades honored and celebrated a victorious Roman general for his military success. In the same way, dramatic irony fills the narrative as Jesus is crowned as the Roman victor in His suffering. Jesus goes to the praetorium, and a cohort of Roman soldiers await Him (15:16). This is the group who would be escorting a Caesar's victory. They adorn Jesus with a purple garment that would be placed on a Roman general after conquest (15:17). Jesus is mocked with praise (15:18–19) and taken to Golgotha, the place of a skull (15:22). Then Jesus is offered wine (15:23), as a triumphator would be offered wine. Finally, He is crucified between two thieves and declared to be the new Sovereign. He cries out to His Father who has forsaken Him, and the temple curtain is torn in two as the heavens were torn open at His baptism. Access to God comes only through blood. A centurion recognizes Jesus' triumph and declares He is the Son of God (15:39).

Jesus' Life (16) / The Servant-King has now suffered and died. It would be a tragedy if the story were over. But this story is just beginning. Unlike the rest of the gospels, Mark's account of the resurrection is filled with mystery and fear. He continues to let the reader watch events from the front row. Some women go to anoint Jesus in the tomb, but when they arrive the stone is rolled away. An angel declares He has risen. But they don't see Jesus. They run in trembling and astonishment. They are afraid (16:8). This strange ending invites readers into Mark's story to imagine how they would react. Mark asks, "How will you respond to this powerful yet suffering resurrected king?"

LUKE

SAVIOR OF
THE WORLD

Luke's message is good news
for the poor.

He has particular interest in the upside-down nature of the kingdom. Jesus is the Savior of the world: this includes women, the underprivileged, and the ethnically marginalized. Unlike Matthew, Luke is concerned with dates. He places the events in the widest possible social and political context. Unlike Mark, who has Jesus rushing about, Luke writes an orderly account where Jesus moves deliberately toward His goal—the cross. Jesus is declared innocent by Rome, yet He is still crucified. His passion and exaltation install Him as Savior of the world.

The early church compared Luke's gospel to an ox—a symbol of divine strength. The ox was a beast of burden, and Luke emphasizes the journey and sacrifice of this burden bearer. Luke opens with a lowly beginning. He recounts the birth of both John and Jesus and also provides temple stories of Jesus' childhood (1–2). Jesus is then baptized and tempted as the Son of God like Adam (3–4). Jesus' ministry begins in Galilee with Jesus proclaiming Jubilee for the oppressed and revealing His identity (4:14–9:50). Luke's largest section concerns the ox's long and slow journey to Jerusalem, where the famous Good Samaritan, Prodigal Son, and Zacchaeus narratives occur to inspire discipleship (9:51–19:27). Finally, Jesus enters Jerusalem as the sacrificial animal. It is necessary for Him to die, rise, and ascend to be the Savior of the world (19:28–24:53).

LUKE / SAVIOR OF THE WORLD

Birth Stories 1-2

Joy results from John's and Jesus' births.

Preparation 3-4

The new Adam is anointed and conquers.

GALILEE 4-9

Jesus announces and performs release in Galilee.

JOURNEY 10-19

Jesus journeys toward Jerusalem, teaching His disciples.

JERUSALEM 19-24

Jesus enters Jerusalem for trial, death, and exaltation.

Good News 4:14-8:3

His message is for the poor and oppressed.

Discipleship 9:51-13:21

He instructs them what it means to follow Him.

Readiness 17:11-19:27

He tells the disciples to be ready for His return.

Passion 19:28-23:49

He is crucified, declared innocent; the curtain tears.

Revelation 8:4-9:50

He is the Messiah from God, but must die.

Warnings 13:22-17:10

He warns them against the world's vices.

Exaltation 23:50-24:53

He rises, appears to many, and ascends to heaven.

Birth Stories (1–2) / Luke is a chronicler of salvation history. His preface declares his aims and sources (1:1–4). Unlike the other gospels, he introduces Jesus through the paired birth stories of Jesus and John the Baptist. Jesus appears as the humble one to exalt the lowly. The narrative pairs characters, first Zechariah and Mary and their songs of praise. Joy fills the narrative at the realization that God is reversing the order of things through this child. Jesus will satisfy the hungry and send the rich away empty. These songs preview the salvation Luke will further expand upon in the narrative (1). Jesus is born in the days of Caesar Augustus, who attempts to assert his power by census. But this too will be turned over. Caesar is contrasted to lowly shepherds who are the first to visit this Savior. Luke brings his readers back into the temple as the aged Simeon and Anna prophesy over Jesus. He is a light to the Gentiles, the redemption of Jerusalem. Jesus is later found in His Father's house, introducing the theme of Sonship, which the next section will pick up (2). Jesus understands His identity; His mission is about to be clarified.

Preparation (3–4) / Luke's second section again pairs John the Baptist and Jesus (3:1–20; 3:21–4:13). But he also places these events in a larger context of Roman and Jewish history and rulers (3:1–2). It was during the reign of Tiberius Caesar, while Pontius Pilate was governor that John came onto the scene. Like the other gospels, Luke positions the Baptist's ministry in the context of a new exodus, but he is the only one to include "and all flesh will see the salvation of God." Return from exile was not only for Jews, but for Gentiles and the poor. John's message is a forceful warning to Abraham's children and foreshadows John's and Jesus' demise. Jesus is baptized, and Luke gives a seventy-seven name genealogy from Jesus all the way back to Adam, son of God. Jesus is the universal Savior, the new Adam. This new Adam is tempted in the wilderness to abandon His sacrificial task as the Son of God, but He withstands the onslaughts (4:1–13).

GALILEE (4–9)

Jesus' inaugural Jubilee sermon in Nazareth encapsulates His ministry. In Nazareth, Jesus reads from Isaiah, saying He has been anointed (christ-ed) by the Spirit to proclaim good news to the poor. This good news concerns release, redemption, and Jubilee for the outcast (4:16–30). The rest of the Galilee narrative illustrates how Jesus proclaims freedom and reveals His identity. He drives out demons, heals, calls and trains disciples (men and women), welcomes centurions, and raises the dead. He condemns the rich and the religious leaders while eating with sinners and tax collectors. Jesus' parables prove the Word will be accepted only by some. Peter then confesses that Jesus is the Messiah and Jesus is transfigured before the three disciples, but they don't understand that this means that Jesus must take up His cross.

Good News (4:14–8:3) / The keynote speech for Jesus' ministry comes in 4:18–19. Jesus does not say repent, for the kingdom of God is at hand, as in Matthew and Mark; He quotes from Isaiah, claiming He is the Spirit-filled Christ figure who proclaims release to the captives, the blind, and the oppressed. This is the same kingdom message, but with an emphasis on Jubilee release. The ox will bear their burdens as their Savior and prophet. Therefore, Jesus heals and casts out demons for the marginalized. His kingdom ministry means welcome for those on the outside. However, His prophetic task also brings opposition. No prophet is accepted in His own hometown. He compares Himself to Elijah and Elisha, who both healed those outside Israel: the widow at Zarephath in Sidon and Naaman the Syrian. This leads to conflict with the Pharisees (5:17–6:11). Then Jesus presents the upside-down nature of the kingdom, telling them to love their enemies (6:12–49). The good news for the excluded is accentuated with a final section on the marginalized (centurion, widow's son, sinful woman) receiving Jesus' message (7:1–8:3). The year of Jubilee has arrived in Jesus.

Revelation (8:4–9:50) / Jesus' message is clear; now His true identity is revealed to the disciples. He begins with parables showing there will be different kinds of responses to Jesus' message (8:4–21), and then He performs extraordinary miracles (8:22–56). Jesus' disciple group extends past the twelve; women are included. Peter climactically confesses Jesus is the Messiah, the Son of God (9:1–20). However, Jesus must die. His message to the poor and His vocation cohere, for His destiny is to be numbered with the transgressors and the marginalized. Jesus must lower Himself like those to whom He ministers. He will become poor and the one who is cast out so He might be the Savior to all. The disciples and the current generation misunderstand this sacrificial mission, so Jesus transfigures before Peter, John, and James, showing them that the only way to exaltation is through suffering (9:31). They need to be trained more in Jesus' discipleship program and this is exactly what Jesus will do in the central part of Luke.

JOURNEY TO JERUSALEM (10–19)

The ox lumbers toward His sacrificial end in the Holy City. This is Luke's famous travel journey with his most unique material. In 9:51, Jesus sets His face toward Jerusalem. Two other times, this phrase will occur (13:22; 17:11), but many other reminders follow (10:1, 38; 18:31; 19:1). The focus on the journey is apprenticeship, as Jesus shows His disciples the gospel is for the oppressed and how He is the Savior of the world. The first section focuses on Discipleship 101 and what it means to follow Jesus (9:51–13:21). The next block warns them about counting the cost, not becoming proud, and trusting God rather than money (13:22–17:10). In the last leg of the journey, Jesus speaks of the coming kingdom, encouraging them to receive the kingdom like a child and trust in Jesus' saving power (17:11–19:27). The journey to Jerusalem is the path to becoming Jesus' pupil as He walks toward death.

Discipleship (9:51–13:21) / Though Jesus' entire journey to Jerusalem concerns discipleship, there is a particular focus on this theme in the first section. The first episode shows Jesus rejects any type of ethnic superiority. He explains to His disciples that following Him will mean giving up much (9:51–62). Jesus then sends out the seventy to proclaim His message (9:51–10:24). Jesus instructs them how to live as His disciples (10:25–11:13). This means loving their neighbors, being taught by Jesus, and learning to pray. The famous Good Samaritan story unifies this section as Jesus teaches them who their neighbor is. Controversy arises with Jesus' opponents (11:14–54), and He warns His disciples against hypocrisy and riches (12:1–34). They must be ready for His return: interpreting the signs of the times and repenting. He will divide households. Though the kingdom seems small now, it will grow into a huge tree (12:35–13:21). Following Jesus means loving God and one another, and this includes the oppressed.

Warnings (13:22–17:10) / The middle section of Jesus' journey to Jerusalem continues the theme of discipleship but focuses more on warnings. Central in this section is the parable of the prodigal son. It showcases the different responses people can have to the Father's kindness. Jesus says they need to strive to be on the narrow path, and then He laments over Jerusalem's negative response (13:22–35). His followers must not be like those who seek the best seats; they should be clothed in humility. They must not be like those who are invited to the banquet, but do not come. Jesus reframes what it means to follow the Sabbath and argues it will be costly to follow Him (14:1–35). Though they might be offended, Jesus' ministry is one of welcoming those on the highways and hedges, the lost sheep, and the prodigal son (15:1–32). He eats with sinners. He came for the sick. He seeks those who have spurned Him, but humbly return to Him. The final warnings concern money (16:1–31). Jesus' followers must not be those who are unjust, who love mammon, nor like the rich man who neglected Lazarus. The kingdom is for those who give, not for those who seek to gain.

Readiness (17:11–19:27) / The final part of Jesus' discipleship teaching on His slow lumber to Jerusalem is centered on the coming kingdom. He promises them the kingdom of God is already in their midst, but it is also still to come. They must be like the persistent widow, the humble tax collector, and little children to enter the kingdom (17:11–18:17). Repentance, perseverance, and humility mark kingdom citizens. They should not be like the rich young ruler holding on to his wealth but like Zacchaeus, who repents and gives to the poor. Salvation comes to Zacchaeus's house (19:1–10). The emphasis on the rich and poor is a consistent drumbeat of Luke. Jesus again predicts His death, showing His own humility, and He heals a blind man, again welcoming the poor (18:31–42). These act as embodied performances of His teachings as He urges meekness. The kingdom is here and is coming; they must be ready, for He is willing to welcome all. The rich, proud, and powerful will have the most difficulty. But there is still hope for those like Zacchaeus.

JERUSALEM (19:28–24:53)

Jesus finally enters Jerusalem as both a passive victim and a potent victor. The conflict has been heightening. Largely positive responses made up the introduction (1–4), Galilee had some opposition (4:14–9:50), the journey to Jerusalem had more (9:51–19:27). Now Jerusalem crucifies its Savior. It is necessary for Jesus to bear not only the burdens of Israel, but the whole world. The passion and exaltation of Jesus climaxes the various themes in Luke's gospel: discipleship, women, outcasts, the poor, and prayer. The gospel commences with a prayer in the temple, and concludes with a prayer in the garden and rejoicing in the temple. Luke opens with a focus on women, and closes with a message from women about the resurrection. Luke begins with the poor, and closes with the disciples on the beach eating fish with Jesus. Luke starts declaring John the Baptist paves the way for forgiveness of sins, and closes with a command from Jesus to preach forgiveness of sins to the whole world.

Entry & Passion (19:28–23:49) / Jesus enters Jerusalem and immediately is confronted with various questions and hostilities. He is asked about where He gets His authority, if they should pay taxes to Caesar, and details about the resurrection. But He confounds the religious leaders with His own questions (20:1–21:4). He then predicts the destruction of the temple and warns them concerning the future (21:5–38). Jesus' farewell speech takes place with His disciples on the Passover, when He tells them Judas will betray Him and Peter will deny Him. They must prepare for opposition (22:1–38). Jesus is then arrested and put on trial, but is declared innocent by Pilate (23:4, 14, 22), Herod (23:15), the thief (23:40), and the centurion (23:47). The centurion, rather than saying He is the Son of God as in the other gospels, says He is truly righteous. Luke's point is that Jesus is innocent. Jesus is crucified as the sacrificial ox between two criminals, but His concern is for those He has always cared for: the lowly, the poor, and women.

Exaltation (23:50–24:53) / Luke ends in a unique way. Unlike Mark, where the women run in fear, and unlike Matthew, where the disciples are climactically sent off, in Luke, Jesus is found in a very human and normal way: walking, eating, and continuing to instruct His friends after His resurrection. Women come to the tomb and they are reminded of the necessity of Jesus' sacrifice but also His resurrection. They report it to the men, but the men don't believe the women's "idle" tale. Two more "normal" people see Jesus on the road to Emmaus and He opens their eyes to Him as they eat with Him. Then Jesus appears to His disciples and they touch Him and eat a meal with Him. He instructs them that this is a new beginning. The message of repentance and forgiveness of sins through a Savior is to be proclaimed to the whole world by the Spirit. Jesus then ascends into heaven. He blesses them as a priest who has entered the presence of God. The story ends as it began: in the temple. Jesus has born their burdens; now they are to do the same for the world.

JOHN

GOSPEL OF GLORY

John's gospel
soars with splendor.

It begins before time. Before light and darkness. Before creation. The easy style and surface simplicity of John's gospel conceal the depths and profoundness of his writing. Jesus is the new creation, wine, bread, water, temple, well, shepherd, teacher, and Lamb of God. John offers stories not told in the other gospels. He uses the phrase "eternal life" more than "kingdom." He argues Jesus is the Word (*Logos*) become flesh. He fills out the picture of Jesus through images and symbols. Like a ladder, John lifts Jesus up to the heavens. But many will misunderstand. So John beckons, "Come and see."

The early church compared John to an eagle—he ascends to heights unknown as he tells of Jesus' glory. John does not shy away from stating his purpose: he writes so people might believe Jesus is the Son of God, and by believing in His name we might have life (20:31). He divides his narrative into two sections: the Book of Signs (1–12) and the Book of Glory (13–20). In the Book of Signs, Jesus transforms the meaning of four Jewish traditions and feasts (2–10). Then comes the ultimate sign: Lazarus is raised from the dead, foreshadowing Jesus' death and resurrection (11–12). The Book of Glory begins with Jesus washing His disciples' feet (13), giving His farewell discourse (14–16) and High Priestly Prayer (17). Then Jesus goes to His death, His glory. He is the sacrificial Lamb. But He is raised up, appears, and reinstates the disciples who misunderstood Him (18–20). Jesus is the Son of God, the King of glory.

PROLOGUE 1:1-5

John the Baptist 1

Passover Meal 13

Jewish Traditions 2–4

Word Made Flesh

Farewell 14–17

Jewish Festivals 5–10

Passion 18–19

Foreshadowing 11–12

EPILOGUE 21

Glorification 20

PROLOGUE (1:1–5)

Mark begins with John the Baptist's ministry, Luke rewinds to the Baptist's birth, and Matthew goes all the way back to Abraham. The gospel of John outdoes them all. He takes a quantum leap back to time before time. He writes on a different plane than the other gospels. The life of the Son is the life of the cosmos. In the beginning the Logos was with God, and the Logos was God. All things were created through the Logos. John picks up resonances from both Jewish and Greek traditions and combines them with Lady Wisdom (Prov. 8:22–31). However, the Logos now has become a human being. Jesus is God's Word, and in Him was life and light. Creation was also an act of life and light, but now John shows his readers it *was* always and *is* only about Jesus.

John the Baptist (1:6–51) / The narrative turns to John the Baptist, but only in the sense that he is a forerunner and witness to Jesus. This Logos swoops down to earth. He became flesh and made His temple on the earth and John has seen Him. Jesus broke the barrier between heaven and earth; He came to dwell on the earth for the sake of the earth. The light came into the world, but the world did not receive Him (1:9–18). John is Elijah, the one who prepares the way; Jesus is the Lamb, who takes away the sin of the world. But the world can't see Him. The motif of misunderstanding punctures the narrative and will continue. John witnesses the Spirit descending on Jesus and confesses Jesus is the Son of God (1:19–34). John's witness leads to others following Jesus (the disciples), even though some doubt (1:35–51). Jesus assures them He is the ladder to heaven, which Jacob saw. He is the new branch and fig tree of Israel.

Jewish Traditions (2–4) / Jesus' signs show He is the Son of God. He encounters four Jewish traditions (jars, temple, rabbi, well) and transforms their meaning, displaying He is the reality to which they all point. The old has gone, the new has come. These signs are performed so that people will believe in Him. First, Jesus goes to a wedding party, where seven jars for ritual purification become containers for new wine (2:1–11). No longer will the old purification rites be needed; the abundant new wine of the kingdom has come as Isaiah predicted (Isa. 25:6–8). Second, Jesus clears the temple with a whip (2:13–25). Jesus is the new temple; no longer do they need the building to meet with God, for they can see God in the person of Christ. Third, Jesus confounds the rabbi Nicodemus, showing He is their one teacher (3). They don't need more information; they need to be born from above. Finally, Jesus goes to a sacred well and displays He is the true and living water (4). He is the source of eternal life to all living in deserted places. The old jars, temple, teaching, and sacred wells could not provide true life. This only comes in the Son of God, who is the Logos.

Jewish Festivals (5–10) / John continues his portrait of Jesus through images and symbols. Jesus is also superior to four Jewish feasts (Sabbath, Passover, Tabernacles, and Hanukkah). Jesus' actions and words toward these festivals produce conflict. On the Sabbath, Jesus heals a lame man who has been afflicted for thirty-eight years. The leaders are upset, but Jesus claims He is the Lord of the Sabbath and has come to do the work of God, making Himself equal with God (5). During the Passover, He provides bread for five thousand, displaying Himself as the new Moses and the true bread of life. If they eat of Him, they will have eternal life. But many are offended at this (6). At the Feast of Tabernacles, where Jews would gather to remember God's provision in the wilderness by water and light, Jesus declares He is the true water of life, the light of the world, and the good shepherd. Some believe, but others are offended at this (7:1–10:21). The final feast story is Hanukkah (Festival of Dedication; 10:22–42). Historically, this celebrated the rededication of the temple by Judas Maccabeus in 164 BC. As Jesus enters the temple, they ask Him if He is the Messiah, the new Maccabeus. Jesus says He is much more than this. He is the sanctified one; He is from the Father, and the Father is in Him. He is the Son of God. This makes the Jerusalem leaders furious, and they plot to kill Him.

Foreshadowing (11–12) / Antagonism has been increasing. Now Jesus' final sign solidifies definitive division. Jesus raises Lazarus from the dead, foreshadowing His own death and resurrection. Jesus' body must also go into the ground to sprout new life. He is the resurrection and the life. However, the leaders gather and plot how to kill Him (11). Jesus goes to Bethany, where He is anointed for His burial (12:1–8), and then on to Jerusalem. His entrance causes division. Some praise Him, while others plot to kill Him. Jesus says this is all according to the Father's will. The Son of Man came for this hour, to be glorified and lifted up. Life comes through death. He came into the world to draw all men to Himself, to repel the darkness, to save the world. If they believe in Him, they believe in the Father. But the leaders are blind, for they love the glory of man more than the glory of God. They love the darkness rather than the light (12:9–50).

Passover Meal (13) / The Book of Signs covered several years of Jesus' ministry. The next seven chapters describe Jesus' last twenty-four hours: the last night and Jesus' final words with His disciples. The Book of Glory slows down the narrative and considers Jesus' death and preparation for His death. In the Passover meal with the disciples, John does not recount the institution of communion, but instead tells about Jesus' washing of the disciples' feet. Jesus becomes a common servant, showing them how He will cleanse them (13:1–20). This not only sets the stage for His betrayal and departure, but symbolically pictures Jesus' death as a cleansing ritual. Jesus is their servant, who washes them by His blood. They must follow Him in this example. They must become servants to all as they watch Him cleanse the world through water and blood (13:21–30).

Farewell Speech (13:31–17:26) / As Jacob, Moses, Joshua, David, and Paul gave farewell addresses, so does Jesus. However, these figures did not come back. Jesus will rise from the grave and send the Holy Spirit so He can always be with them. Jesus assures, comforts, and consoles His disciples in light of the coming difficulties and His departure. Hardships will come when He leaves, but they need to be full of love for one another and trust Him. He is the way, truth, and life. They need to understand the nature of Jesus' mission: His death, exaltation, departure, and the subsequent gift of the Paraclete. The Spirit will be with them forever. The Spirit will teach them all things, bear witness to Jesus, guide them into all truth, and convict the world concerning sin and judgment. The unity and love of the triune God is applied to the disciples. Jesus is the true vine, and they are the branches, so they must abide in Him (14–16). In His High Priestly Prayer, Jesus asks that God might be glorified in Him, that His followers might be sustained and preserved from evil, and that all might come to glory (17).

Passion (18–19) / The hour of glory has now come. John's entire narrative paints Jesus' death as a Passover sacrifice. Jesus is the Lamb of God, who takes away the sins of the world. Jesus is in full control as the Scriptures are fulfilled in His death. The story begins and ends in a garden (18:1; 19:41). Jesus is betrayed in the garden, but affirms He must drink the cup the Father has given Him to establish the new garden-city. In the garden, He declares His final "I am" statement, and the soldiers who have come to arrest Jesus fall backward (18:1–14). Jesus willingly goes to His death. He then goes to trial before the high priest and Pilate, declaring His kingdom is not of this world. He is not after their power; He is a servant to all (18:28–40). Peppered between these narratives is Peter's threefold denial of Jesus. All have now abandoned Jesus. Finally, Jesus is lifted up on the cross and the sign on the cross declares to the entire known world that Jesus is the King of the Jews (19:19). Even on the cross, Jesus cares for His mother. As David cried out, Jesus says, "I thirst." As the Scriptures predicted, His clothes are left intact. Like the Passover lamb, none of Jesus' bones are broken; His side is pierced instead. Water and blood flow out to the world.

Glorification (20) / On the first day of the new age, Mary Magdalene comes to the tomb. She finds it empty and tells the disciples. They also find the tomb empty. In John, Jesus appears to whom He wishes. First, He shows Himself to Mary. Mary stays in the garden weeping, and she sees who she thinks is the gardener. But it is Jesus tending His new creation. He tells Mary He is to return to the Father, He will not stay. But He will send the Spirit (20:1–18). Second, Jesus appears to His disciples declaring peace to them and breathing the Holy Spirit upon them. This is their commission (20:19–23). Third, Jesus appears to Thomas. Thomas was not with the disciples when Jesus came; he doubts until he is able to touch Jesus' scars. So Jesus appears to Thomas and says, "Do not disbelieve, but believe" (20:24–29). Jesus' resurrection compels belief.

EPILOGUE (21)

The epilogue is likely written by another author. In it, Jesus appears one more time to His disciples, back at their old profession: fishing. They don't recognize Him at first, like Mary and Thomas. But Jesus reveals Himself. Jesus has foresight to fill their nets with fish. They will also be fishers of men as they listen to Jesus' voice and direction. Peter is then restored from his threefold failure with a threefold command to feed Jesus' flock. But Jesus also has foresight about the kind of death Peter will die. Rumors of what happened to Jesus' body are circulated, but the author notes John's testimony is true. Jesus is the Lamb of God. He is the Word become flesh. He is the Lord of glory.

ACTS

TO THE ENDS
OF THE EARTH

Within the space of thirty years,
the gospel traveled from Jerusalem to Rome.

It was preached in the most splendid, formidable, and corrupt cities. It had touched the Holy City (Jerusalem), the City of Philosophers (Athens), the City of Magic (Ephesus), and the empire (Rome). Its message and work were not done in a corner. Its victory and opposition were not brushed over. Acts recounts the story, struggle, and success of the gospel message going forth, all under the plan of God, centered on King Jesus, and empowered by the Spirit. The triumph of this movement cannot be attributed to the apostles or Paul, but only God Himself. From an earthly perspective, "the change brought about by the twelve apostles is the most inexplicable, mysterious, and wonderful event that has ever been witnessed in this world. This can only be because God attended it."*

Luke writes to encourage the church, telling them *this* is the plan of God. God's kingdom scheme is not put on hiatus once Christ leaves; it simply kicks into a different gear. Jesus ascends, the Spirit falls, and Jesus' witnesses are sent to Jerusalem (1–7), Judea and Samaria (8–12), and the ends of the earth (13–28). Peter receives most of the focus in the first half, while Paul's journeys take up the second half. The narrative ends with Paul on trial and in prison. But the word about the King and the kingdom is not bound. It continues to spread.

---

* Albert Barnes, *Notes, Explanatory and Practical, on the Acts of the Apostles*, 10th ed. (New York: Harper, 1851), vi.

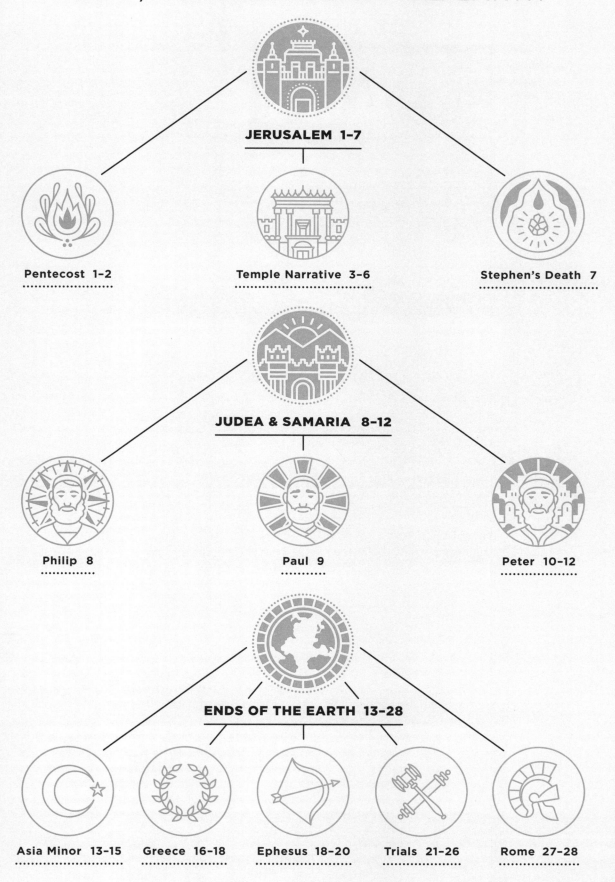

JERUSALEM 1–7

Pentecost 1–2

Temple Narrative 3–6

Stephen's Death 7

JUDEA & SAMARIA 8–12

Philip 8

Paul 9

Peter 10–12

ENDS OF THE EARTH 13–28

Asia Minor 13–15

Greece 16–18

Ephesus 18–20

Trials 21–26

Rome 27–28

JERUSALEM (1–7)

It all began in Jerusalem. Geography is essential to Acts. It is from a specific place the witnesses are empowered by the Spirit and sent forth to the rest of the world because it is through Israel that the world will be blessed. More specifically, the beginning narrative focuses on the temple. Jesus ascends to the true temple in heaven, His people receive the Spirit, becoming mobile temples on the earth, and they go into the temple spreading the resurrection life of Jesus (3–6). However, the temple leaders oppose them, arrest them, and tell them to stop speaking of Jesus. But they won't stop proclaiming what they have witnessed. Finally, Stephen is killed for his words about the temple (7). A new epoch has come. The question becomes: Will those who hear this message recognize that Jesus fulfills their hope or reject the promised Messiah?

Pentecost (1–2) / In Acts 1–2 Luke recounts *how* God establishes His new community. Before Luke gets to main events, he recounts the apostles' commission: they will be witnesses by the power of the Spirit to Jerusalem, Judea and Samaria, and to the ends of the earth (1:8). The following narrative pattern closely follows the promises made in the prophets: the Davidic king is enthroned (1:9–14), Israel's twelve tribes are reunited (1:15–26), the exiles are gathered from the nations and the Spirit is poured out on the new people of God (2:1–13). Pentecost imagery paints the people as the new temple, the home of the divine being. Peter's sermon interprets all these events looking back to the Old Testament (2:14–41). They now live in the last days, for the Spirit has come and Jesus has been glorified. Three thousand people repent. A new Spirit and Torah community has been formed (2:41–47). Resurrection life is here.

Temple Narrative (3–6) / The witnesses are the new mobile temples, but they clash with the temple leaders. The narrative recounts two temple resurrection stories (3:1–10; 5:12–16) paired with opposition from temple leaders, which provides opportunities for sermons about Jesus' resurrection (3:11–4:31; 5:17–42). Between these temple narratives are key panels that describe the true people of God, focusing especially on how they use their money (4:32–5:11; 6:1–7). Antitheses fill the narrative: the home is contrasted to the temple, the church leaders are juxtaposed with the temple authorities, and Satan's plan (death) is opposed to God's plan (life). The importance of the temple abides, but the temple was never meant to restrict the presence of God. Persecution catapults the spread of God's Word as sermons puncture the narrative. The last note Luke gives in this section is, "And the word of God continued to increase, and the number of the disciples multiplied greatly in Jerusalem, and a great many of the priests became obedient to the faith" (6:7). God's purposes are accomplished through His servants as the temple space expands.

Stephen's Death (7) / The Jerusalem cycle and its emphasiś on the temple comes to a climax in the narrative concerning Stephen's trial, speech, and death by stoning. Opposition has been escalating. Now a witness is martyred—but even this leads to more expansion. Stephen is accused of disrespecting the temple and law, and responds with an argument about the temporary nature of the temple and the rejection of God's prophets through history. Stephen stands in the long line of righteous sufferers: Abraham, Joseph, Moses, and Jesus Himself. Stephen's speech displays God as unable to be contained within the temple. Jesus now stands in the true temple in heaven, and Stephen sees Him as he dies. *Stephanos* (which means "crown") rightly will receive the crown of life because of his death. Stephen's death and sermon are foundational for the geographical expansion of God's temple presence. New life will sprout from the seed of Stephen's blood.

JUDEA & SAMARIA (8–12)

The glory of the temple will no longer be restricted to Jerusalem. Nor will the apostles be as tightly tied to the narrative. God propels His witnesses to those on the margins, thereby unifying the earth under the reign of the heavenly Christ. The heavenly entourage is unmistakably active in this section: people are transported, visions occur, the Spirit speaks. Readers first hear of Philip's mission to Samaria and the conversion of an Ethiopian eunuch (8:4–40). Luke then recounts the call of Saul, who becomes the key missionary to Gentiles (9:1–30). Peter has a vision and encounter with Cornelius, which authorizes the Gentile mission (9:31–11:18). Everything before leads to Peter's vision, and everything after provides the results. The "Gentile Pentecost" pivots the book of Acts, and the rest of the narrative will detail more fully this Gentile welcome. Cornelius's narrative leads to a multiethnic church in Antioch, which becomes the mother church for the Gentile mission (11:19–30). Finally Peter leaves Jerusalem because of persecution (12:1–25).

Philip (8) / Philip's narrative should be viewed under the geographic banner of Jesus' words in 1:8. The word extends from Jerusalem to Samaria (north) and Africa (south). Both Samaritans (8:4–25) and the Ethiopian (8:26–40) are outcasts and have an uncomfortable relationship with the temple: Samaritans rejected the Jerusalem temple and eunuchs could not even pass the court of the Gentiles. But God refused to be bound by temple obstacles. The Lord declared He would gather the dispersed of Israel and still others "besides those already gathered" (Isa. 56:8). The largely successful mission to Samaria reunites the people of Israel and conquers the powers of darkness. With the eunuch, the energetic Spirit guides Philip to cross temple and geographic boundaries. He welcomes the eunuch to the temple people through baptism. Now the treasurer of the south becomes a treasurer in the house of God.

Paul (9) / Saul has already been introduced as the great enemy of the church, but now in a moment of great reversal, his apocalypse of the ascended Jesus installs him as the great missionary of the church. The narrative emphasizes that Paul's Gentile mission was God's idea, initiative, and achievement. Paul is called to bear Jesus' name to Gentiles, kings, and Israel (9:15). He stands as the second branch that stems from the seed of Stephen's blood. Paul goes from light to darkness and back to light. He will bring light to the Gentiles, but this will also bring much darkness and persecution to him. Paul's apocalypse becomes a key episode in Acts. He is commissioned to the Gentiles as a prophet of old who beholds the glory of Christ.

Peter (10–12) / All of Acts has the Spirit on the move, pushing people to share the good news. This particular section has Peter meeting three individuals in ascending narrative length: Aeneas, Tabitha, and Cornelius. In the first section, Peter ministers in Lydda and Joppa with resurrection power (9:32–43). In Joppa, Peter receives his vision to go see Cornelius and in Caesarea is convinced that Gentiles are no longer unclean (10:1–11:18). Cornelius is the first Gentile that Peter will share table-fellowship with, thus indicating his acceptance into the new community. Luke makes this abundantly clear by slowing down the narrative and essentially telling the same story three times. It is God who compels the church to take this step, the Spirit who legitimates, and the Son who is revealed; Peter and the church are reluctant participants. The narrative has been building up to this point and now ministry in Jerusalem will move into the background as Gentiles become brothers and sisters by the reception of the Spirit.

ENDS OF THE EARTH (13–28)

Paul is not the central character moving forward. It is still the triune God who spreads the light of the temple to the ends of the earth through His servants. Paul was chosen to bear *the name of Jesus* to Gentiles, kings, and the sons of Israel (9:15). Now readers will find out how the mission is accomplished. The advent of a new order has arrived in the urban imperium. As God's servants travel to the nations, they are continually called back to Jerusalem, indicating this mission is still *from Jerusalem*. The geographical focus persists, but fans out—to Asia Minor, Greece, Ephesus, and Rome. Though Caesar claimed rule over the inhabited world, a new ascended King was reclaiming territory with a message of peace. The emphasis in this section is not only on the carrier or object of the good news, but the response of both Jews and Gentiles to the Word. Reactions get violent, but these are not petty outbursts of anger; rather, they are tremors of the quake Paul delivers.

Asia Minor (13–15) / In Paul's first journey, Luke gives snapshots and cameos of the different obstacles and success the missionaries encounter. However, he shows Christianity is superior to syncretism (Cyprus), and has a superior Savior (Antioch), gift (Iconium), and deity (Lystra). On Cyprus, Paul and Barnabas encounter cosmic conflict through a Jewish sorcerer, but a prominent Gentile ruler comes to faith (13:1–12). In Lystra, they are confused for gods, but instruct the crowd to turn from their empty gods to the living God who created all things and offers hospitality to them unlike the capricious gods they worship (14:8–20). Between Cyprus and Lystra lie Pisidian Antioch and Iconium, where Luke provides the message of a superior Savior and gift. They report back to the sending Antioch church that God has opened the door for Gentiles to come to faith. This leads to the Jerusalem Council (15), where the leaders in Jerusalem affirm Gentiles can be welcomed without following the Torah. This movement also has superior unity.

Greece (16–18) / In Paul's second journey, a divine vision of a Macedonian man pushes him and his companions farther west. They therefore head closer to Rome, where they will encounter unique challenges and continue to argue for a superior household (Philippi), king (Thessalonica and Berea), philosophy (Athens), and virtues (Corinth). In the Roman colony Philippi, three unique conversions ensue. Paul and Silas end up incarcerated (16:6–40). In Thessalonica and Berea, they announce a new King, but some think this upsets the current political order, causing more upheaval (17:1–15). Paul enters Athens and acts as a well-trained philosopher who declares the resurrection of the dead (17:16–34). Finally, they trek to Corinth, where the Way is declared innocent of wrongdoing (18:1–17). The section shows the gospel's impact on the Greco-Roman world as Paul and his companions preached the message of the ascended Lord. Paul's gospel was a culturally destabilizing force that threatened religious beliefs, social cohesion, and political stability. The new age has come in the body of Jesus. Luke therefore highlights the culture-shaking and culture-forming power of Paul's message.

Ephesus (18–20) / Ephesus was one of the most important and largest cities Paul evangelized and was known for its magical practices and the Artemis cult. If in Athens Paul shows Christianity is a superior philosophy, in Ephesus he proves that the forces of darkness and magic can't overpower the name of Jesus. The narrative thus becomes the conclusion and capstone of Paul's work as a free man. The Ephesus story also puts the Jesus movement alongside other groups: disciples of John (18:24–19:7), Jewish exorcists (19:8–20), pagan shrine makers, and government officials (19:21–41). Though the city officials find this movement innocent of charges, Paul's message conquers idols, magic, and paganism. In contrast, charity is extended to John the Baptist's followers. The Way has inherent resources to address all worldviews it encounters.

Trials (21–26) / Though Paul has traveled many miles, his eyes have increasingly been set on Jerusalem and Rome. Finally, he enters the Holy City—although like Jesus, he is not welcomed but arrested. Luke spends significant time on Paul's trials, making this the final and climactic trial of the Way. The Sanhedrin (23), Governor Felix (24), Governor Festus (25), and King Agrippa (26) all question Paul. Luke continues to portray the Father's plan as being fulfilled, despite adverse circumstances. Paul is Jesus' witness before Jews, Gentiles, and kings. The trials prove the innocence of Christianity in relation to both Judaism and Rome. Though Christianity fulfills Judaism, it also stands in continuity. Though Christianity collides with the current political structures, it is still innocent of sedition and Jesus does not seek Caesar's throne. In fact, Paul can even appeal to Caesar, confident that his message is untainted.

Rome (27–28) / Many stories enjoy tying all the loose ends together. Others leave things unfinished for readers to meditate on their involvement. In some sense, Luke does both. He concludes by recounting Paul's journey and arrival to Rome, closing that loop. However, in another sense he leaves things half finished. The book ends with Paul in a Roman prison. This shows Luke's narrative is not about Paul or Peter primarily, but about their message. Nothing can hinder the unfolding of God's plan—not storms, shipwrecks, or snakes (27). Paul continues to act as God's prophet, even though he is imprisoned (27–28). Paul is also shown again to be righteous and innocent, thus vindicating his Gentile mission. He has been declared innocent by the Roman court and will continue to affirm his commitment to Judaism, but now God and nature speak. The last words of Acts tell of how, despite Paul's imprisonment, he proclaims the kingdom of God with all boldness and without hindrance.

ROMANS

RIGHTEOUSNESS OF GOD

Caesar's shadow was long, but the shadow of the cross unites communities.

Though Rome was the world power, Jesus is the true King, and His embassies infiltrated the empire. Paul had never been to Rome. Yet he writes to this diverse community, detailing how the gospel unifies Jews and Gentiles. At the heart of the letter is the theme: the righteousness of God. Paul asserts that God's goodness, justice, and faithfulness is revealed in his gospel. It is by trust in the Messiah—and not works of the law—that all people are made right with God. Therefore, Paul's gospel is for both Jews and Gentiles. By declaring this unifying message, Paul subverted the divisions of the world, creating a new community of love and peace.

Romans begins with Paul's thesis: the gospel is God's power for all people because in it the righteousness of God is revealed. The righteous will live by faith (1:16–17). The rest of the letter expands on the revelation of righteousness. First, Paul shows God's wrath is revealed against all unrighteousness of Jews and Gentiles (1:18–3:20). Then Paul explains how righteousness is declared through the death and resurrection of Christ and people obtain it through faith like Abraham (3:21–4:25). This results in hope (5:1–11; 8:31–39) and life in the Spirit (8:1–30), because Jesus has triumphed over Adam's sin (5:12–21), which leads to freedom from sin and the law (6–7). But how can God be righteous and faithful if so many in Israel have not responded? Paul defends God's righteousness in 9:1–11:36, arguing that Israel was disobedient. But God still has a remnant within Israel and promises to save Israel. Finally, Paul turns to righteousness displayed, urging Roman believers (both Jews and Gentiles) to offer their bodies as living sacrifices to God (12–15).

ROMANS / RIGHTEOUSNESS OF GOD

Thesis   1:1–17

The gospel displays God's righteousness.

DENIED   1–3

All have sinned and stand under the wrath of God.

Gentiles & Jews 1:18–3:8

Gentiles have sinned; Jews have broken the law.

Under Sin   3:9–20

No one is righteous; all have followed the snake.

DECLARED   3–4

Christ's atoning death makes the unrighteous righteous.

HOPE   5–8

Those justified by Christ have hope in trials.

DEFENDED   9–11

God is righteous and faithful in His plan and choosing.

Abraham & Faith   4

Abraham believed God and was counted righteous.

Freedom   5:12–8:17

Jesus triumphed; freedom from sin and law results.

Remnant   11

Israel's rejection not complete; a remnant will return.

DISPLAYED   12–15

Righteousness means offering bodies as living sacrifices.

World   13

Submit to the government; love fulfills the law.

Church   14–15

The weak and strong are to love one another.

Conclusion   15:14–16:27

Paul's travel plans, commendation, and promise of hope.

Thesis (1:1–17) / Paul commences by declaring he is an apostle for the gospel of God. This gospel was promised in the Old Testament, centered on Jesus, and summarized in the phrase "Jesus is Lord." He wants to visit Rome so that they may encourage one another with spiritual gifts. In 1:16–17, Paul presents the thesis for his entire letter. He affirms that though both Jews and Greeks have opposed him, he is not ashamed of the message he preaches. In this message, the resurrection power of God is made known. More specifically, the righteousness of God is given to those who have trust in Christ from first to last. It is entirely by faith, from the beginning to the end. Though this message includes Jews and Gentiles, it was given to the Jews first, then Gentiles. Gentiles have been grafted onto the olive tree. Paul already foreshadows the end of his letter, where he will call for unity between the weak and the strong.

RIGHTEOUSNESS DENIED (1–3)

The body of Paul's letter begins with the bad news: all have sinned (both Jews and Greeks) and therefore stand under the wrath of God. They have denied God's righteousness in their actions. Gentiles are guilty because though God has made Himself known through creation, they have worshiped what God has created rather than worshiping Him. They are idolaters (1:18–32). But Paul surprised his audience. Jews are also guilty (2:1–3:8). Though Jews have the law, they have not followed it. They condemn themselves as they practice the very things they accuse Gentiles of. Therefore, both Jews and Greeks are under sin and the wrath of God (3:9–20). All have sinned and deserve the justice of God.

Gentiles & Jews (1:18–3:8) / Paul begins with the sentence passed on Gentiles, and then moves back to explain the grounds of this verdict. The wrath of God is upon Gentiles because they have ignored the truth about God. They are without excuse. Like Adam and Eve, Gentiles traded the truth about God for a lie (1:18–32). This is a retelling of Genesis 3–11. They began to worship created things rather than the Creator. As a result of rejecting God, they are given over to their own destruction. The spiral of sin and selfishness saturates their lives. The lusts of their hearts rule them. Dishonorable passions control them. A warped mind leads them. Sin leads to more sin and the sentence is just. But Jews are in the same boat (2:1–3:8). They might think they are superior to Gentiles, but Jews have not kept the Torah. So how can they judge their neighbor? In judging, they actually condemn themselves. God shows no partiality. Jews who judge are no better off. They have advantages, but these advantages simply prove their unrighteousness.

Under Sin (3:9–20) / Paul brings his argument to a head, arguing all humanity has listened to the voice of the snake. They are trapped and guilty before God. Jews and Gentiles are both condemned by the weight of sin. God will judge the entire world since there is no one righteous, not one. All are under sin. The Old Testament affirms there is no one who seeks God, no one who does good. The influence of the serpent has been effective far and wide. This is evidenced in the evil that has taken hold of humanity. Blood, cursing, war, and lying follow in their train. Every human is guilty before the judge, who is God Himself. By works, no one will be justified before God. The law gives knowledge of sin and highlights the transgression of mankind.

RIGHTEOUSNESS DECLARED (3–4)

However, God's righteousness has been revealed climactically in Christ (3:21–31). God's response to sin is the provision of forgiveness and righteousness through His very own Son. Jesus' sacrificial atonement reveals the justice of God. God becomes both the just (He punishes sin) and the justifier (He declares people righteous) in the cross and resurrection. Those who trust in Jesus (both Jews and Gentiles) are welcomed into Abraham's family. In fact, Abraham was promised an innumerable family line. This entrance into the family is a gift, not a result of works, because it is by faith. The implication for both Jews and Greeks is that there is no ground for boasting. None have earned their standing, for all have sinned. This doesn't overthrow the law; it upholds it. Abraham is the father of the faith, and the promise of a large family was made to him (4).

Abraham & Faith (4) / To prove his point about the nature of faith and the harmony between Jews and Gentiles, Paul recalls the story of Abraham. Abraham was declared to be righteous before he was circumcised, not after. Abraham's story proves justification is by faith and not works (4:1–8). He was *declared* righteous. It was not what was due to him because of his works. His faith preceded his circumcision. Abraham is thus the father of all people (4:9–15). Circumcision is a sign of faith, not a rite that brings about faith. Abraham believed God could give life to the dead. He had hope in the impossible, that God could give his and Sarah's old bodies a child (4:16–22). Abraham's story is for all people who have faith that Jesus is the crucified and risen Lord. The Romans who have faith in the God who raises the dead have the same faith of Abraham. He is the father of both Jewish and Gentile faith.

RIGHTEOUSNESS AND HOPE (5–8)

Paul turns to the future hope for those of faith, those of Abraham's family. People who are right with God inherit promises. Since they have been justified by grace, they have peace with God. Suffering doesn't mean they are not God's children; God uses their suffering to mold them into the creatures He wants them to be. Hope does not disappoint. Those who believe in the Messiah have a secure future (5:1–11). They have hope because they have freedom. Jesus is the new Adam who defeats sin and death. They are also free from the law since a new era has arrived (5:12–8:17). Paul returns to the subject of hope and suffering in chapter 8. The present sufferings are not worthy to be compared to the inheritance coming for them. A new creation is coming; the Spirit gives them the hope that they will reach their destiny. Nothing can separate them from Christ's love, not even death (8:18–39). Nothing can defeat their hope, not even the worst of trials.

Freedom (5:12–8:17) / This hope is founded on the freedom Christ brings. Jesus' family is a new kind of humanity. Adam introduced sin and death, but Christ (the new Adam) announces grace and life. Jesus' triumph results in freedom and hope. Jesus' work overwhelms, overpowers, and overcomes Adam's. The death of Adam is swallowed up in Christ's victory (5:12–21). His faithfulness leads to freedom from sin, and sin no longer has tyranny over them. They are no longer slaves to its power, for they have been transferred to a new allegiance in their baptism. They have died with Jesus and been raised with Him (6). In the same way, they are free from the law. The law made sin increase, but that doesn't make the law sin. It simply demonstrates the sinfulness of sin. The law was good in its time, but a new era in Christ has arrived (7). Though sin and the law stood in their way, now they have freedom by the Spirit. The Spirit enables them to fulfill the Torah. They are not of flesh, but of God. They are led by the Spirit as sons of God (8:1–17).

RIGHTEOUSNESS DEFENDED (9–11)

This is all good news, but doesn't the lackluster response of Israel raise questions about God's faithfulness and righteousness? Paul climactically defends God's righteousness, arguing God has been faithful to His promises to Israel even though some of Israel does not believe. There has always been an Israel of the flesh and an Israel of the promise. Ethnicity never automatically made one a member of God's family. Jacob and Esau are prime examples of this reality. Jacob was chosen, Esau was not. God is still faithful to spiritual Israel. Paul stands as an example of spiritual Israel. The Israel of flesh has stumbled over Jesus and not submitted to righteousness from God that comes by faith. Yet Israel still has the opportunity to believe as the gospel message is brought to them, and Paul promises there is a remnant of Israel who will be saved on the last day. These realities should humble both Gentiles and Israel and not make them proud over their brothers and sisters.

Remnant (11) / The rejection of Israel is not complete nor final. Paul affirms the call of Israel that cannot be recalled or revoked. There will be a surprising twist at the end. God has not rejected His people. He will save those whom He foreknew. God has chosen a remnant to be saved, and there will be a future day for Israel even though right now a majority of them are hardened. Israel stumbled so that Gentiles could come in, but this will only make Israel jealous. Gentiles should not be proud because they have been grafted onto the olive tree as wild shoots. If they can be grafted on, they can be cut off. Paul affirms that at the end, a large number of Jews will come to Jesus. God's righteousness has been defended. His wisdom is beyond what humans can perceive and too wonderful for them to comprehend.

RIGHTEOUSNESS DISPLAYED (12–15)

Paul transitions from his theological magnum opus to instructing those in Rome how to embody God's righteousness as a unified covenant community. They are to present their bodies to God as living sacrifices, to employ their gifts for the benefit of others, spreading love and goodness, and nonretaliation. They are also to demonstrate their righteousness in the world, submitting to the government and fulfilling the law by loving others. Finally, they are given instructions concerning the weak and the strong, particularly in relation to food. He calls on them to not judge, not cause stumbling, to help the weak, and to have love for one another because Jesus accepts all.

World (13) / Living in Rome as a Christian was not easy. How were they to continue in the faith in a world hostile to their faith? Paul must address the path for God's people in a pagan culture with regard to political authorities. He affirms something surprising. They are to submit to the governing authorities in Rome. They are to avoid two extremes: an over-realized kingdom view that ignores Caesar and an under-realized kingdom view that thinks they need to pick up their sword against Caesar. The "third way" is that a new age has dawned, and they should submit to their authorities because God has installed them (13:1–7). To fulfill the law, they are to love their neighbor and be good citizens (13:8–10). The hour is coming soon when Christ will return and they need to be ready by doing good works (13:11–14). They are living in the new Babylon and must seek the peace of the city.

Church (14–15) / In their own local congregations, the Christians in Rome are to display righteousness and unity. After eleven chapters of dense theology, Paul's longest exhortation is this: have people over to eat and don't argue about secondary things. Paul's theology paves the way for harmony. The central issue is table fellowship and the observance of certain days. Disunity was arising because of competing views on observing the Torah in Rome. Paul says these practices don't define who is in and out of the church family. Paul does not want the church to divide over such things, so he tells them to welcome and love one another and refrain from judging (14:1–12). The "weak" are mainly law-observant Jewish Christians who want to eat kosher, while the "strong" are mainly nonobservant Gentile Christians who believe a new era has arrived. Paul urges them to not cause another brother or sister to stumble (14:13–23) and to help the weak (15:1–6). Ultimately, they need to accept one another, for Gentiles are partakers of God's family (15:7–13).

Conclusion (15:14–16:27) / Paul closes by speaking of the goal of his mission (to preach the gospel where Christ has not been named) and his desire to visit them before he goes to Spain. He commends Phoebe, who delivers the letter, and sends his greetings. He closes with this promise: the God of peace will crush Satan under their feet. Previously they were conquered, but Christ subjugated the serpent, and now the church participates in God's triumph. God has declared victory in Christ even in the midst of the Roman Empire. Soon only one kingdom will stand.

1 CORINTHIANS

UNITY & PURITY

The message of Jesus
transforms every corner of life.

Corinth is a church filled with chaos and confusion. Divisions, sexual immorality, lawsuits, table-fellowship problems, and disorderly worship fill the church. Some are sleeping with temple prostitutes; others are saying all sex is wrong. Greco-Roman values were hard to shake off. Yet Paul still declares they are sanctified in Christ Jesus. Jesus' death and resurrection is the pattern for God's holy people as they mature in unity and purity. Paul begins showing how the cross unites them and concludes with a reflection on their resurrection hope.

The first letter to the Corinthians is different from any other letter Paul writes. Rather than a prolonged argument, it reads topically, as if he jumps from one short essay to the other. He responds to oral reports (1–6) and written reports (7–16). He addresses issues that center on ecclesiology (1–4), morality (5–7), liturgy (8–14), and theology (15). However, there is continuity to these issues as well. Embracing Roman values results in conflict (disunity) and compromise (impurity). So, Paul urges them to live as saints. They need to put away all divisions (1–4), sexual immorality (5–7), and disordered worship (8–10). They are to put on love and hope (11–15). The gospel applies to every area of their lives: from who they sleep with, to what they eat and what they wear.

1 CORINTHIANS / UNITY & PURITY

Sanctified   **1:1-9**

The Corinthians are holy and have gifts.

Divisions   **1-4**

The foolishness of the cross brings unity to factions.

Immorality   **5**

A man has his mother-in-law; he must be removed.

Lawsuits   **6:1-11**

Rather than suing each other, they should be unified.

Marriage & Singleness 6-7

Don't excuse sexual immorality, and live as called.

Food & Idols   **8-10**

An ethic of love controls eating food offered to idols.

Worship   **11**

Celebrate gender distinctives and have unity in the Eucharist.

Gifts   **12-14**

All have gifts. Use the gifts to build up and love one another.

Resurrection   **15**

Jesus was raised with a new body, and believers will be too.

Collection   **16**

Paul is returning to collect the money for Jerusalem.

Sanctified (1:1–9) / Though there are problems in Corinth, you would never know it by the way Paul begins. He speaks of their unity, set-apartness, and thanks God for their evident faith. The Corinthians are God's holy people. They are God's new community. God's grace is evident in their lives. Their gifts of speech and knowledge are demonstrable. No spiritual gift is lacking in them. Yet interestingly he does not mention their love, which comes up frequently in Paul's thanksgiving for other churches and becomes a big part of this letter later on. He does encourage them, saying Jesus will strengthen them and keep them pure till the day He returns. The theme of the letter is evident even in this thanksgiving. The Corinthians are the unified people of God whom Jesus will keep unblemished.

Divisions (1–4) / Paul received a report that there were factions forming in the church. Different personalities (Apollos, Cephas, Paul) were dividing the congregation. The Corinthians were following the wisdom and values of the world rather than of Christ (1:10–17). However, the economy of God is evidenced not in eloquence but in spiritual wisdom. He gives a few examples. First, God's upside-down method is displayed in the foolishness of Christ crucified. God confounds the wise with this foolish message. This is God's wisdom and power (1:18–25). Second, the very makeup of the Corinthian congregation shows that God's wisdom is displayed in the weak and ignoble. God chose the foolish, the weak, and the insignificant to turn the world upside down (1:26–31). The third demonstration of God's economy is Paul himself. Paul came with much weakness and trembling and didn't seek to impress them with his skills (2:1–5). Therefore, the wisdom the Corinthians latch on to is not wisdom that comes from above (2:6–16). All of God's workers are cruciform servants. It is God who gives the growth; not Apollos, Paul, or Cephas (3:1–4:21). The congregation needs to repent of their divisions because the cross is the power and wisdom of God. Boast in God, not His servants.

Immorality (5) / Though the Corinthians view themselves as spiritual (for they practice many gifts), Paul takes the wind out of their sails in this next section. Are they so puffed up that they continue to accept a man who is sleeping with his mother-in-law? This sinner corrupts their assembly like leaven leavens a loaf of bread. The church's holiness in Jesus Christ compels them to drive out this wicked person. They need to cleanse themselves and deliver this man over to Satan. Their boasting about their gifts is not good when they continue to allow gross sin in the church. They need to remove the leaven (the wrongdoer) from their household (Ex. 12:15), which will mark them out as distinct. Jesus Christ is their Passover Lamb who has died to cleanse them and mark them out as God's people. They must live into who they are in Christ. They must rid their community of overt, public, and rebellious immoralities.

Lawsuits (6:1–11) / The theme of judging continues, but now it is applied to inappropriate judging. Paul scolds the Corinthians for trying to settle disputes in civil courts rather than deciding these things internally. Their disunity is put on display to the world when they sue each other and fight in local courts. In so doing, they fail to take responsibility for one another like in the previous section. They fail to be the church God called them to be. Saints will judge the world and yet they allow unbelievers to judge them in court. This is doubly wrong because those of high social status would usually win in court. Money buys friends and freedom. Paul has already shown how God has chosen the weak and later he will rebuke them for not waiting for the poor when they eat. The gospel solution is to not wrong and cheat each other. They need to be unified. God has washed and sanctified them; they need to deal with matters internally.

Marriage & Singleness (6–7) / Paul now tackles a variety of topics around marriage and singleness. He first responds to their claim "all things are lawful for me." Likely, they were arguing sexual desire is like an appetite that can be satisfied at any time, even with temple prostitutes. But Paul says no! Their bodies were made to glorify God, and God intends to resurrect their bodies. God owns their bodies, so glorify God with them. Sexual partnership is not a matter of indifference (6:12–20). On the opposite end, there were those who thought sex was always wrong. But Paul says it is a gift for married couples. They should have sex (7:1–7). Next he goes through a situational list, giving advice to those finding themselves in a variety of circumstances. Widows are to stay unmarried (7:8–9), Christian couples should not divorce (7:10–11), Christians married to unbelievers should also not divorce (7:12–16). The main principle is to stay as you are called (7:17–24), and this applies to single Christians as well. In fact, Paul puts a high value on singleness, saying that those who are single can uniquely devote themselves to the Lord (7:25–40). Readers should remember that Paul is addressing specific situations, not producing a marriage manual. Yet he also covers a number of topics. His main point is this: lead the life God has assigned and honor Him with your body.

Food & Idols (8–10) / Corinth was a city filled with gods, temples, and shrines. New converts would face a variety of situations where they wondered what was proper. One of the primary places this came up was about food. Should they eat food sacrificed to idols? What if someone else was offended by this? Paul's answer is complex. In 8:1–13, he argues for an ethic of love concerning temple food. Even if they have knowledge that temple food is permissible since there is only one God, love should rule the day. They should not put a stumbling block before those who would find offense to eating idol food. He urges them to limit their freedom for the sake of their brothers and sisters. Paul himself has freedom, but he sacrifices it for others. He has the right for financial support, but he refuses. The Christian life is not for self-gratification, but discipline and love (9:1–27). Paul then argues there is another compelling reason to not eat food offered in the temple. In so doing, they engage in idolatry, especially if they eat idol food in the temple (10:1–22). In summary, believers should only do what is helpful, edifying, and beneficial to other believers. In the privacy of their own homes, they are free to eat, but in public, they should refrain (10:23–11:1).

Worship (11) / Paul now turns to the worship gathering. There seems to have been some gender distractions in the assembly. Paul argues that the distinction between men and women has been ordained by God. These distinctions should be reflected in the dress and hairstyles of believers. In this culture, this meant head coverings and long hair for women. Both of these signs distinguished men from women. These differences should be celebrated, rather than downplayed, because of the creation order. Men and women are unified and interdependent, like the Trinity. However, both the Trinity and creation also reflect a dissimilarity. Therefore, men should not cover their heads in worship, but women should. A second issue for the congregation was that food was not getting distributed evenly at the Lord's Supper. It seems the wealthier members were eating and the poor were being deprived. Paul says Jesus' table is for unity, not division. No VIP cards are needed at this table, so they should welcome one another. When they eat together in unity, Jesus' harmonizing death is proclaimed. They contradict Jesus' self-sacrificing death when they discriminate against the poor.

Gifts (12–14) / The Corinthians are confused about the nature, importance, and proper exercise of spiritual gifts. The meeting had become chaotic. Paul explains that the same Spirit bestows different gifts to benefit the church (12:1–11). The same source means all gifts are spiritual, and no gift is unimportant. Paul confirms this by comparing the different gifts to the various abilities of different members of the human body (12:12–31). He then urges them to cultivate a better way, the way of love in chapter 13. Love is more important than any exercise of spiritual gifts. If they have gifts but do not have love, they have nothing. However, they are to still desire the higher gifts: prophecy and tongues. Prophecy is to be preferred even more than tongues because it builds up the community, while tongues only builds up the individual unless there is an interpreter. Ultimately, he encourages order and edification in the congregation.

Resurrection (15) / Paul's final topic concerns the resurrection of the dead. Some questioned, under the influence of Greek culture, their own resurrection. How can an earthly body that is perishable be raised? Paul says Christ's resurrection is the blueprint and their hope. Jesus' conquering of death is central to the gospel. Without it, the entire message collapses. Jesus' resurrection is verifiable as well; He appeared to many after His death. If Christ has been raised, then others will be raised with Him. This is possible because the perishable body will put on the imperishable. Their bodies will change. They will be given a heavenly body that will be raised in glory. If Adam came from the dust, then the risen Christ came from heaven. We too will bear a heavenly body, which is also physical. Christ has conquered death. His victory is their victory. Their future is full of hope.

Collection (16) / Paul closes with instructions, his travel plans, and a final exhortation. He tells them that when they meet, they should set aside money for the Jerusalem church. Jerusalem was suffering under a famine, and Paul was going back around to the churches to collect money for this needy church. The Gentile congregation was to provide for the Jewish congregation. He plans to revisit them in Corinth, but he will stay in Ephesus until Pentecost because the gospel is going forth. He may send Timothy and Apollos ahead of him to check on them. He closes with an exhortation to stand firm and do everything in love. They must resist disunity. They must be characterized by love. They must be holy. In fact, they already are.

2 CORINTHIANS

STRENGTH
IN WEAKNESS

The foolishness of the cross. Treasures in jars of clay.
The aroma of death. Boasting in beatings.

Paradoxes fill Paul's second letter to Corinth. If in Romans one saw Paul's theology, here Paul bares his heart. He wears it on his sleeve, not hiding his affection, anger, or agony. Paul defends his ministry, arguing his suffering, weakness, and change of travel plans don't disqualify his ministry. They actually qualify him. His hardships display God's power. He boasts in God's strength in his weakness because through his weakness the power of the gospel is displayed. The gospel message turns the world upside down.

The sustained defense of Paul's ministry arises because certain false teachers (super-apostles) have infiltrated Corinth, claiming Paul is a farce, and many in the church were convinced by them. Still, the majority in the church have repented, and thus the major note in chapters 1–7 is Paul's joy over their repentance. From the outset of the letter, one of the major themes of the letter is struck: suffering leads to the comfort of others (1:1–11). Paul explains that he didn't visit them because he didn't want to cause them pain (1:12–2:13) and explains his bold new covenant ministry. They behold His glory with unveiled faces (3:7–18). Paul then requests that Corinth finish the gift they have been collecting for Jerusalem (8–9), which will be proof that they are reconciled to Paul. Finally, Paul changes his tone in the last three chapters. He asserts his authority to those who refuse to be reconciled to him (10–13).

2 CORINTHIANS / STRENGTH IN WEAKNESS

Suffering & Comfort   1:1–11

Paul's afflictions lead to comfort for believers.

PAUL'S INTEGRITY 1–7

He acted toward them with simplicity and sincerity.

Absence   1:12–2:13

He didn't want his visit to cause pain.

Ministry   2:14–7:4

His glorious ministry resides in jars of clay.

Titus's Report   7:5–16

Titus reports the good response to Paul's letter.

PAUL'S REQUEST   8–9

The expected contours of obedience are outlined for them.

Collection   8–9

Paul comes to collect money for the Jerusalem church.

PAUL'S DEFENSE 10–13

Those who reject Paul's ministry are now addressed with force.

Authority   10:1–11

Paul will be bold; he tears down strongholds.

Boasting   10:12–12:13

He is forced to boast in his strengths and weaknesses.

Third Visit   12:14–21

He comes seeking their hearts, not money.

Warning   13

Those who reject Paul will not be spared.

Suffering & Comfort (1:1–11) / Paul begins by reestablishing his relationship with those in Corinth. His change of travel plans seems to have put a strain on the relationship. People were attacking him because of his suffering, travel plan alterations, lack of rhetorical eloquence, and his request for the collection of money. The opponents said Paul is weak, he doesn't even care for them, and he wants their wealth. Therefore, Paul defends his suffering, explaining to them that persecution and weakness is purposeful. It enables him to draw on comfort from God and pass it on to others. He is not hiding his suffering, which is likely the thorn in his flesh. He wants them to be aware that his affliction is for their benefit. He hopes they will accept him, even though his ministry reeks of death.

PAUL'S INTEGRITY (1–7)

Paul is happy with the Corinthians' response to him, but he still defends himself in light of the false teachers. His argument is that his conscience is clean. He acted toward them with simplicity and sincerity. He did not require money from them, and he was honest with them (1:12–14). In regard to his travel plans, he asserts that he was not vacillating. He did not say yes and no. Rather, he didn't come so as not to cause them pain. But he was worried when Titus was not found at Troas (1:12–2:13). He then defends his ministry in terms of its superiority (2:14–4:6), its suffering and glory (4:7–5:10), and appeals to them for a response (5:11–7:4). Finally, he recounts to them Titus's happy report about how the Corinthians long for Paul, and therefore his letter was effective (7:5–16).

Absence (1:12–2:13) / Paul defends his absence from Corinth. One day they will boast in him, as he will boast in them. Three reasons exist why Paul did not come to Corinth as originally planned. First, he says he was not of two minds, sometimes saying yes and other times no. His ministry is modeled on the faithfulness of God in Jesus Christ, who is God's yes (1:15–22). Second, Paul did not travel, because the trip would have caused them pain, likely a severe scolding (1:23–2:11). Finally, his care for them is proved in that when he went to Troas he moved on quickly. A door for the gospel was open, but Titus was not there, which caused him unrest. Titus was supposed to bring news of how Corinth received Paul's "severe letter." So Paul quickly went to Macedonia to hurry his journey to them, showcasing his deep affection (see 2:12–13).

Ministry (2:14–7:4) / The attacks on Paul display a distorted value system. Paul's weakness and boldness stem from the gospel and his new covenant ministry. Even though some might accuse him because of his severe letter, Paul has an authentic ministry of suffering and boldness in the Holy Spirit. The two go together. For example, Paul is led like a prisoner of war toward his death, spreading the aroma of Christ's death. He doesn't want to be impressive; he wants to point them to Jesus (2:14–3:6). However, he also has a bold ministry of the Spirit. While Moses had a glorious ministry, Paul's is even more glorious and bold because his face is unveiled (3:7–4:6). But this covenant treasure is contained in "jars of clay." A glorious and bold ministry resides in an inglorious, weak, and suffering receptacle. Paul's ministry carries Jesus' death in his body, but it is for their life. He has a powerful but cruciform ministry. But he has hope because his body will be raised from the dead (5:1–10). Finally, he appeals to them for a response. His life stands open before them (5:11–15). He is a minister of reconciliation, so he pleads with them to be reconciled to God (5:16–6:2). He has been open with them. He hopes they will open their hearts to him as well (6:3–7:4). They are only reconciled with God if they are reconciled with Paul.

Titus's Report (7:5–16) / Paul returns to where he left off in 2:13. He didn't find Titus in Troas, so he was concerned about how they had responded to his previous letter. Now Titus has brought back an encouraging report of how they are doing. They long for Paul, mourn over their sin, and have zeal for Paul. Even if his previous letter made them grieve, it was effective. It produced godly repentance rather than worldly sorrow, which has in return produced fruit in their lives. Therefore, Paul is comforted because of Titus's report. He rejoices because he has complete confidence in Corinth. Their past actions give him hope for the future. His weak but bold ministry has been effective with them.

PAUL'S REQUEST (8–9)

Paul transitions to his request: a gift for the Jerusalem church, which suffers under a famine. This is not an aside; rather, it details the contours of obedience that Paul requires. A failure to give reveals a failure of their hearts. Did his previous letter really produce fruit? The response to this gift will disclose their hearts. He connects this giving to the gospel. Jesus also became poor for them; Paul has become poor for them. This was so they might become rich. Now they need to become poor in imitation of Paul and Jesus. The paradox of poverty turning to wealth is evident. Therefore, he exhorts them to finish the collection (8:1–15). This is why he sent Titus to them (8:16–9:5). Finally, he lists the reasons for giving generously: God will bless them if they do (9:6–15). Release leads to return and reward.

Collection (8–9) / On the topic of the collection, Paul begins with an example for Corinth to follow. The Macedonian churches (north of Corinth) have given to the Jerusalem church in the midst of affliction. But Corinth has forgotten to save for this gift. This is why Titus came to them: to complete this act of grace. While they excel in spiritual gifts, he hopes they will also excel in giving too. He asks this of them to prove the genuineness of their faith. Titus has personally devoted himself to this mission of collecting the money. Paul sends him so that Paul's boast about Corinth might not prove empty. They need to give because if they do, God will reward them. God loves a cheerful giver. He blesses givers. God has given them the greatest gift. How could they not give a gift as well?

PAUL'S DEFENSE (10–13)

Paul certainly had concerns in the first part of the letter, but now his unease takes a new turn. Gone is the affirmation and encouragement. Now Paul addresses those who persist in rejecting his ministry: the false teachers and their followers. Before he gave encouragement to those who might have questions but still accepted his ministry and responded well to his letter. Paul wanted to encourage the faithful majority. Now he censures those who reject him. He forcefully addresses the super-apostles who think his ministry is nothing. His hammer comes down on them with power. His ministry is not weak, but bold and full of strength. They will see the potency of Paul.

Authority (10:1–11) / The false teachers declare Paul is bold in his letters, but weak in person. If Paul is away, he will write Corinth a strong letter but while he is with them, he is weak. Paul contends his meekness is not weakness. Though he might look or sound feeble, he is dealing with supernatural realities and tearing down strongholds. He defeats armies of darkness. He wages war in another realm and will come with boldness and confidence if he has to, wielding his apostolic authority. If they think his letters are strong and his presence is weak, he will show them what true power looks like when he returns and disciplines the disobedient. They haven't seen power yet.

Fool's Boasting (10:12–12:13) / The super-apostles boast in their credentials. Paul is forced to as well. He says if they want to compare, his résumé far exceeds theirs. He calls it foolishness to do so, but Corinth must bear with him. But he will only boast in what God has done through him. He asserts he is not inferior to the super-apostles. They think he is an inferior speaker, but he has knowledge. They think he is not worth his salt because he did not require money from them, but he did this to care for them. These super-apostles are the ones who should be on trial. They are deceitful servants of

Satan. Since they boast in the flesh, he is driven to boast as well, but to his shame. He is a Hebrew, a son of Abraham, a servant of Christ. But then he shifts to boasting in his weaknesses. He has been through more labor, more imprisonments, countless beatings, often near death. He was even given a thorn in his flesh, but Jesus said to him, "My power is made perfect in weakness" (12:9). Therefore, Paul would rather boast in his weaknesses since God makes him strong through suffering.

Third Visit (12:14–21) / Paul asserts he is coming for a third visit. He seeks not the Corinthians' money but their hearts. He seeks their souls, not their gold. He will gladly lay his life down for them, but if he does so, will they hate him for it? Will they only see weakness as he comes to them with the aroma of death on him? He has not taken advantage of them. Neither has Titus. He has defended himself so that they might be built up, not so he might feel better about himself. He is afraid that when he comes to them, he might not find them as he expects to. If so, he will come with authority and discipline the recalcitrant. He is committed to them. Will they commit to him and avoid future discipline?

Warning (13) / Paul concludes with a warning. He addresses the whole congregation, but concentrates especially on the rebellious. If the rebellious are still there, he will not spare them. He will come with the power of Christ. Christ died in weakness, but He was raised in power. Paul will come with both the weakness and power of Christ. He looks at the repentant and encourages them to test themselves. Jesus Christ is in them! He hopes they have not failed the test. Paul is weak for their sake that they might become strong. He is Christ embodied to them: strength in weakness.

GALATIANS

FREEDOM IN CHRIST

Nothing can be added to the gospel
of the crucified Messiah.

Paul's passion and pastoral heart are on display in Galatians as he rebukes false teachers and clarifies his gospel. Some were claiming circumcision and observance of the law was necessary for Gentile believers to become members of God's covenant people. Paul contends they preach a different gospel. A new epoch has arrived in Christ. Both Jews and Gentiles are free in Christ. They live by the Spirit, not by the flesh. Dualities resound throughout Galatians: God-humanity, Spirit-flesh, freedom-slavery, and Christ-law are all opposed to one another.* According to Paul, circumcision means nothing; Christ means everything.

Paul essentially tells a series of stories to support his point—stories about himself, Christ, the Galatians, and salvation history. He begins by defending his own authority to validate his message (1–2), then gives a series of arguments for justification by faith both from experience and biblical history (3–4), and finally argues they have freedom in Christ by the Spirit (5–6). The Galatians don't need to submit to circumcision, the Jewish calendar, or dietary customs. Jesus has come. He is the fulfillment of all Israel's hopes. They can live in freedom by the Spirit.

---

* John M. G. Barclay, *Paul and the Gift* (Grand Rapids: Eerdmans, 2015), 338.

GALATIANS / FREEDOM IN CHRIST

No Other Gospel   1:1–10

Paul chastises the Galatians for turning to another gospel.

PAUL'S AUTHORITY 1–2

Paul's gospel was derived from God, not people.

JUSTIFICATION   3–4

The Scriptures show justification comes by trust in Jesus' death.

SPIRIT & FREEDOM 5–6

The Spirit grants them freedom to live in love.

Divine Calling   1:11–24

Jesus appeared to Paul in light on the Damascus Road.

Experience & Scripture 3:1–14

Abraham trusted God's promise of a multiethnic family.

Slavery   5:1–12

Paul warns them not to submit to circumcision.

The Pillars   2:1–10

Years later James, Peter, and John confirmed Paul's message.

The Law   3:15–4:20

The law was temporary and imprisoned people under sin.

Led by the Spirit   5:13–6:10

The Galatians need to keep in step with the Spirit, not the flesh.

Rebuke of Peter   2:11–21

Paul even rebuked Peter with his gospel of justification by faith.

Sarah & Hagar   4:21–31

They are children of Sarah (free), not Hagar (slave).

New Creation   6:11–18

People are made righteous by faith, not works of the law.

No Other Gospel (1:1–10) / Paul begins by emphatically identifying himself as an apostle from God rather than humans. This is a key theme that stretches throughout the entire letter and buttresses Paul's authority. Paul's gospel is summarized in verse 4: Jesus gave Himself for sins to deliver people from the present evil age. A new era has arrived in Christ's death and resurrection (1:1–5). He then transitions to what is customarily in letters a note of thanksgiving, but instead he chastises them. There is no thanksgiving. Paul is bewildered they "are turning to a different gospel" (1:6). Later readers find out this is especially in relation to making people take on the marks of the Mosaic covenant. If they add anything to the message of Jesus, it actually detracts from Jesus. Paul doesn't hold back when he says if anyone preaches another gospel, let him be cursed (1:6–10).

PAUL'S AUTHORITY (1–2)

To bolster the certainty of his message, Paul must defend his authenticity and authority. He does so by giving a narrative of his own story, speaking of how his gospel was derived from God, not people. His message was given to him by revelation on the Damascus road (1:11–12), and he did not go to Jerusalem or consult with anyone about it immediately (1:16–17). This means his message comes from divine origin. After three years he did go to Jerusalem to meet with Peter. Very few knew him, and he only saw James in addition to Peter (1:18–24). All the while, he was preaching the gospel independent of the Jerusalem church. Then after fourteen years, he went up to Jerusalem and they confirmed his message. He even rebuked Peter, the rock, with the message of justification by faith alone (2:11–21). This is God's message given to him; therefore it is binding.

Divine Calling (1:11–24) / Paul begins by stating his authority came not from humans, but from God (1:11–12). He supports this by showing his gospel was independent of humans and came by revelation. Christ gave him this message, not Jerusalem leaders. First, he explains that his past life was filled with hostility toward the Way. He is the least likely candidate to preach Jesus after he persecuted Christians (1:13–14). Second, his call came from God through revelation. This was not another stage of his life plan. It was a divine interruption (1:15–17). Finally, he did not go up to Jerusalem immediately but waited three years. When he arrived there, he was an obscure figure and only met with Peter and James (1:18–24). Paul's authority is confirmed because his message had no human origin. It came from God Himself.

The Pillars (2:1–10) / Though Paul's message came from God, Jerusalem affirmed it as well. Fourteen years after his first visit, he went up to Jerusalem and was recognized by the pillars of the church: James, Cephas, and John. His gospel came from God, but Jerusalem also confirmed his ministry. They approved his gospel. Paul tells the story of how he presented his gospel to them in Jerusalem and even Titus was not commanded to be circumcised, even though there was pressure to do so. Jerusalem confirmed his message for Gentiles. However, false brothers came in and tried to circumcise Titus, which Paul labels as submitting to slavery rather than freedom. Later he will return to this language of slavery/freedom in full force. But the pillars backed Paul's gospel of freedom and gave him the right hand of fellowship.

Rebuke of Peter (2:11–21) / The final example of Paul's authority is his rebuke of one of the pillars: Peter. When Peter came to Antioch, he was eating with Gentiles, thus at least presumably abandoning dietary restrictions and separation codes. Certain Jews arrived, and Peter separated himself from Gentiles, fearing what the Jews would think. This led to other Jews also splitting from Gentiles, even Barnabas (2:11–14). But when Paul saw this separation, he confronted Peter with the gospel. He rebuked Peter, saying his actions are contrary to what they preach. It is by faith both Jews and Gentiles are justified and not by works of the law. People are made right with God through trust, not by ritual markers. Paul's whole mission has been to tear down dividing walls between Jews and Gentiles, and Peter's actions betray the gospel. Righteousness does not come through the law but through Christ (2:15–21). Paul's gospel is confirmed in that he even rebuked Peter with it.

JUSTIFICATION BY FAITH (3–4)

In the second section of Paul's letter, he turns from his autobiography and directs their attention both to their own story and the story of the Scriptures. In all this, he expands on his summary of justification by faith through the cross of Christ in 2:15–21. He begins with the Galatians' experience of the Spirit (3:1–5) and then siezes upon a series of scriptural interpretations: Abraham, the law, and Sarah and Hagar (3:6–4:7; 4:21–31). The goal is to show that the Spirit, who began the work in them, is continuing to work not based on adherence to the law but based on faith. Abraham's story, the temporary nature of the law, and the allegory of Sarah and Hagar all support Paul's message. Paul's message came from God, but is in continuity to the Scriptures. To seek circumcision would be to return to slavery. To seek Torah regulations is to go back in time. The cross of Christ frees them.

Experience & Scripture (3:1–14) / Paul begins chapter 3 by calling the Galatians foolish. They are foolish because they need to think back on their own conversion and see that the current teaching is contrary to their experience. They received the Spirit not by works of the law but by faith. Why would they think the Spirit's work would continue by works of the law? It makes no logical sense (3:1–5). Then he turns to Abraham's story, the father of the Jewish faith. People become a part of Abraham's family by trust. Abraham believed before he was circumcised and was promised a large multiethnic family. Those who have his faith are part of the family (3:6–9). On the opposite side, the curse of the law is only removed in Christ and His sacrifice. Faith leads to blessings; the law leads to a curse. But Christ became the curse to open the blessings to Jews and Gentiles (3:10–14). Abraham's large family is being realized.

The Role of the Law (3:15–4:20) / Paul continues with the story of the Scriptures but looks more to salvation history and the relationship between the promises to Abraham and the law given to Moses. If God promised Abraham a multiethnic family, then why was the law given, separating Israel from the nations? He essentially asserts that the law was temporary. The Abrahamic covenant has priority over the Mosaic covenant because it came earlier. The addition of a new law doesn't void the promises to Abraham. And the promises to Abraham concern a multiethnic family (3:15–18). Negatively, the law was given to increase and reveal sin. It magnifies their sin problem and points to Christ. But this doesn't mean the law is contrary to the promises of God, for positively the law was an interim guide, a custodian, a nanny, until Christ came. It had its good purpose until its role was over (3:19–25). For example, a child is subject to guardians until they are grown. They only become heirs in the fullness of time. In the same way, God's people have moved from slavery to the law to sonship in Christ. Therefore, to turn back to the law is irrational; that era is over (3:26–4:11). Paul entreats them to listen to his plea (4:12–20).

Sarah & Hagar (4:21–31) / The final scriptural story Paul gives to support his point about justification by faith is the allegory of Sarah and Hagar. The two women represent two covenants. The two women represent two mountains: Mount Sinai and the Jerusalem above. Hagar the Egyptian is the slave woman, while Sarah is the free woman. Hagar's child is born of flesh, while Sarah's is of the Spirit. As Sarah drove out Hagar, so the Galatians need to drive out teachings about following Jewish customs to be a part of God's family from their midst. They should not return to slavery, for they are children of the free woman. They are children of Sarah and therefore they are free in Jesus Christ. It is not only Paul's authority but the story of the Bible that supports Paul's gospel.

SPIRIT & FREEDOM (5-6)

Though Paul has been juxtaposing slavery and freedom for the entire letter, he turns more specifically to speak about freedom in the Spirit in his final section. The ethical implications come in full force as Paul instructs them to resist slavery (5:2-12) and keep in step with the Spirit (5:13-6:10). The Spirit is the key to freedom. There are two ways to live. The works of the flesh are opposed to the works of the Spirit. One brings life and unity; the other brings death and disunity. The two cannot coincide. Paul closes his letter urging them to press into the new creation. New life is here in Jesus. Nothing else matters. Not even works of the law (6:11-18).

Slavery (5:1-12) / Paul warns them against submitting to the yoke of slavery by undergoing circumcision and adhering to works of the law. If they accept circumcision, then Jesus holds no promise for them. Jesus must be all in all. It must be faith working through love and nothing else (5:1-6). Then he turns to the perpetrators and tells the Galatians they should not listen to those who are troubling them. In fact, if the false teachers require circumcision, he wishes they would go ahead and cut the entire thing off. Paul has no time or sympathy for those who lead the Galatians in the wrong direction. It must be Christ and only Christ (5:7-12).

Led by the Spirit (5:13-6:10) / Rather than submitting to slavery, Paul calls them to live out their freedom in the Spirit with humble love. His message is not just about transformed individuals but transformed communities. Their freedom is not to be used for their own gratification, but to serve others (5:13-15). They need to keep in step with the Spirit, for the desires of the flesh and the desires of the Spirit are at odds. Sexual immorality, idolatry, divisions, strife, and anger are opposed to love, joy, peace, patience, and kindness. These are diagnostic tests telling one whether the Spirit or the flesh is at work (5:16-26). Caring for one another and bearing one another's burdens is a sign of the Spirit, while laying weights on people is a sign of the flesh. They need to support one another, persevere in their own work, and share resources with one another (6:1-10). The Spirit is in the work of creating new communities full of love and peace.

New Creation (6:11-18) / Paul closes by affirming this letter comes from his own authoritative hand. Those who seek to have them circumcised only want to boast in their flesh and not in Christ. But Paul will only boast in the cross of Christ. All that matters is the new creation: circumcision and uncircumcision mean nothing. People are made righteous by faith, not by the works of the law. Paul's story has proved this, the Galatians' own story signals this, and salvation history undergirds this. It is about the cross, not circumcision. They live in the era of freedom by the Spirit.

EPHESIANS

COSMIC RECONCILIATION

The invisible realm is real.

An unseen battle has been raging from the beginning of time. Ephesians soars to heights unknown to the human eye. Paul writes to those in Ephesus telling them the cosmic story of heaven, earth, and the powers. This celestial reality has common consequences. God's cosmic plan should form how they relate to neighbors formed from the dust. What happens in the heavens reverberates on earth. The two realms are linked by the body of Christ.

Paul's argument begins from the widest angle and moves to the most intimate relationships in households. He asserts God's overarching plan is to unite all things in heaven and earth in Christ Jesus. Cosmic reconciliation. This results in new lives, new relationships, new behaviors, new loyalties, and new power. But this all stems from the triumph of Christ over the powers of darkness. Paul transforms their imagination by showing them what God has done for them in Christ (1–3). He then encourages them to embody God's victory by subversive performances (4-6). They stand against the powers in the strength of their victorious King.

EPHESIANS / COSMIC RECONCILIATION

COSMIC 1

CHURCH 2

PAUL 3

Trinity's Work 1:1–14

Dead to Alive 2:1–10

Steward 3:1–13

Prayer 1:15–23

New Temple 2:11–22

Prayer 3:14–21

Unity 4:1–16

PARTICIPATION 4–6

The church participates in the triumph of Christ, living by new standards and in new relationships.

Warfare 6:10–24

New Creation 4:17–32

Households 5:22–6:9

Love & Light 5:1–14

Wisdom 5:15–21

COSMIC (1)

Paul begins with the widest lens possible: before time and in the heavens. By so doing, Paul transforms their imaginations and puts their personal narratives in the larger scope of the universe. The triune God's plan before time was to sum up all things in heaven and earth (1:9–10). He did this through respective actions of each person of the Trinity (1:1–14). This is meant to encourage those in Ephesus in the midst of their daily walk with Christ. After Paul has detailed the cosmic plan, he prays that they would have spiritual eyes to see the beauty and splendor of this mystery (1:15–23). God's plan is to unite all things in the Head and His body.

Trinity's Work (1:1–14) / Praise be to God. That is Paul's main point. He praises God for the work of the Father, the Son, and the Spirit. Their plan is to unite the cosmos in the Son. He begins with the Father's work (1:3–6a). God chooses His people. He chose them for a new vocation and family. They are to be holy and part of His household. They therefore have a new heritage and birthright. This all comes through the Son, the Beloved. The Son's gift is redemption (1:6b–8). By His blood, His people go through the water, receive forgiveness of sins, and the enemy is defeated. This redemption displays that God's plan is to sum up all things in Christ, things in heaven and on earth (1:9–10). If the Father orchestrates and the Son redeems, then the Spirit's gift is His presence as a seal (1:13–14). The Spirit is the down payment of the inheritance. Jews and Gentiles have the same inheritance through the work of the Spirit.

Prayer (1:15–23) / Paul has explained the cosmic plan, and now he prays. They need to have spiritual eyes to see the gifts of the Godhead (1:18). It would be too easy to read over these truths and shrug. So Paul prays. He prays that they would have wisdom, revelation, and knowledge (1:18–19). He prays that their eyes would pierce the darkness so they can see three realities. First, the hope of His calling (1:18). Second, the amazing inheritance that is theirs (1:18). Finally, and most importantly, to know the power that was worked on believers' behalf (1:19–23). Jesus was raised from the dead and seated above the powers of darkness. Christ is the head of creation and the new creation. Christ's power is their power. He is the victorious and triumphant Messiah, who has subjected every other power under His rule. He rules over His church, His body, which is going to fill all things: things on heaven and on earth.

CHURCH (2)

If Paul began with the widest lens, now he focuses on how this cosmic plan is manifested in the church. His prayer in chapter 1 ended with how Christ's body (His church) will fill all things. Now Paul details how this will take place: Jews and Gentiles will become the new creation and temple. He begins with creation imagery: they were dead but are now alive by Christ's victory (2:1–10). Then he transitions to temple imagery, arguing that through Christ's blood, Jews and Gentiles together become the temple that is built on Christ (2:11–22). In sum, he gives both creational and covenantal images. Jesus is both the victorious King and the sacrificial Lamb. Christ's body will fill the earth as they are united under Him.

Dead to Alive (2:1–10) / The body of Christ will fill all creation, but how? Paul explains it is by a work of new creation, a new enthronement, a new humanity. Previously, they were dead (2:1–3). They stood under the powers. The world, Satan himself, and the flesh attacked them, producing God's wrath. But now God has made them alive with Christ, raised them with Him, and seated them with Him (2:4–7). Christ's benefits are their benefits. This all came about because of God's gift, God's blessing (2:8–10). It was not because of their good works, but because of His gift. Therefore, they can now walk in the new creation and the good works that God has prepared for them. Being alive, raised, and seated means they have a new earthly vocation from their heavenly Lord. Cosmic reconciliation is embodied on earth.

New Temple (2:11–22) / The imagery now switches from creation to covenant metaphors. Paul moves from separation of Jews and Gentiles to unity. This only comes through blood. Previously, Gentiles were outside the temple people (2:11–12). They were separated and strangers to the people of God and therefore to God Himself. But they have been brought near through the blood of the Lamb (2:13–18). Those who were far off have been brought near. Those who were hostile to one another now have peace. Those who were antagonistic to God have been reconciled. Christ killed the hostility between these two groups on the cross, bringing them both together as His body. Now they are being made into the new temple (2:19–22). They are no longer strangers and separated, but they are members of God's house. The Ephesian Christians are pillars in His temple, stones in His walls, and growing into a dwelling place for God. Jesus is not only the sacrificial Lamb but also the cornerstone on which this temple people is built. A new temple is being formed where heaven and earth collide.

PAUL (3)

Paul began with a cosmic snapshot, then he moved to a church snapshot; now he turns to his own role in this management of the plan to sum up all things in Christ (3:1–13). The reason Paul is a prisoner is because God has made him a manager and ambassador of God's grace and the revealed secret. He expresses Christ's victory through suffering. This mystery was not made known before; now it has been revealed that Gentiles are partners in the promise of the gospel. This is the uniting of heaven of earth. Paul's role is to proclaim and bring light to this mystery. Even the powers of darkness look at this plan and are amazed. Paul closes this section of the letter with another prayer (3:14–21). He asks for strength in their hearts for God to do exactly what he has outlined.

Steward (3:1–13) / Paul wishes to transition to his prayer for Ephesus in light of the church's role in God's plan, but he must stop and explain why he is in prison. The victory of Christ and his suffering seem at odds. However, Paul's suffering manifests the plan. His life is an example to follow. Suffering is how Paul expresses God's victory. Paul explains his relationship to the mystery (3:2–7) and the mystery's relationship to the cosmic plan (3:8–13). Paul is a steward of this mystery. It came to him by revelation. The content of the mystery is that Gentiles are coheirs, partakers in the promises with Jews. This is a more specific definition of the mystery than in chapter 1, where he argued it concerns all things (on heaven and earth) being summed up in Christ (1:9–10). Paul's role is to shine light on this revealed secret, and that is why he is in prison. Even the powers look down on the church and are amazed at this plan. This is why he is bold.

Prayer (3:14–21) / Paul closes the first half of his letter with another prayer. He pleads for his listeners that they might be able to exemplify this cosmic plan in their lives. In so doing, he summarizes his themes and speaks to how this applies to their lives. He returns to his heaven-and-earth theme, bowing his "knees before the Father, from whom every family in heaven and on earth is named" (3:14–15). Then he prays three things for his readers. First, that they might have strength so that Christ may dwell in them (3:16–18). If Christ's body is going to fill the earth, they will need help to have Him overhaul their lives. Second, they need to know the greatness of the love and power of Christ (3:19–20). To be the new temple will take a reservoir of love that is unending. Finally, he prays that they might be full of God (3:21). God's presence was in the temple, and now they are the temple. Paul prays that the cosmic and theological reality might become a personal reality.

Unity (4:1–16) / The second half of Ephesians details how those in Ephesus can participate in the triumph of Christ. Paul continually returns to "walking" imagery in this section. He first tells them they need to walk in unity, but not uniformity (4:1–6). They are to be unified because their God is one. This unity is already theirs in the Spirit, but they are still to make an effort. This daily exercise stems from Paul's theology of God, the church, and the future. There is one body, one Spirit, one hope, one Lord, one faith, one baptism, one God. But this call to unity does not smother diversity (4:7–16). God has given diverse gifts to His church. When Christ ascended to the right hand of the Father, He distributed a variety of gifts to His church. His ascent should remind them of Christ's victorious descent to the dead. Both His descent and ascent prove Christ conquered all spaces. He gave people as gifts to the church so that they might build a new temple on earth.

New Creation (4:17–32) / Not only are they to embody God's victory by walking in unity but also by walking in the new creation. The old humanity walked in darkness, futility, ignorance, and had no life because of their hard hearts (4:17–19). But that is not the way they were trained in Christ. Through the Spirit they now have hearts of flesh rather than of stone. They were taught to put off the old human and to put on the new human, who is Christ (4:20–24). Jesus is the truth. They are to perform the actions of a new self, according to God's image. They are the new Adams and Eves. Paul then details the virtues of the new human in contrast to the old human (4:25–32). Put off lying, put on truth. Put off anger, put on self-control. Put off stealing, and put on work hard. Put off filthy talk, put on edifying speech. Put off bitterness, and put on a tender heart. These are new creation realties. This is heaven and earth reconciled as God's image shines through His new people.

Love & Light (5:1–14) / Embodying the new creation means walking in love and light. Love reminds people of the two greatest commands; light reminds readers of new creation images. Christ is love and light. This love is most clearly seen in Christ's sacrifice for His people on the cross and is contrasted with self-love. Self-love is defined here in terms of sexual immorality, greed, and crude jokes. All of these vices reveal more concern for oneself than other image bearers. Thanksgiving should replace these corruptions. If they continue in sexual promiscuity, greed, and crude jokes, their end is destruction, the kingdom of darkness, and God's wrath (5:1–6). Chaos and destruction await those who turn from God. But they are no longer in darkness. They are in the light (5:7–14). The kingdom of light consists of goodness, righteousness, and truth. When the true light comes it will expose the darkness. They were once held sway by the powers of darkness, but light has come! Therefore, they must arise, wake up from the dead, and Christ's light will shine on them (5:14).

Wisdom (5:15–21) / Participation in the triumph of Christ also means walking in wisdom (5:15–16). Jesus is the new Solomon, the true, wise King upon whom the Spirit rests. He listened to His Father's instruction, took the narrow path, and chose the tree of life. Foolishness means squandering the time they have in this dark world (5:17). Satan is still the prince of the power of the air, who tempts and accuses them. They therefore need to understand the will of the Lord and be filled with the Spirit (rather than wine) like their wise teacher (5:18). This will result in songs, hymns, thanksgiving, and submission to all (5:19–21). The next section on households is a subsection of the wisdom theme.

Households (5:22–6:9) / Paul applies this wisdom to households. The war for the cosmos takes place on the ground through the interactions of husbands and wives, masters and slaves, and parents and children. This too is cosmic reconciliation. Paul calls on husbands and wives to perform both standard and subversive tasks (5:22–33). Wives are to submit to husbands, and husbands are to love their wives. This model is built on Christ's relationship with His church, His body. Children are to obey parents, so they may partake of the new creation, and fathers are to be kind and gentle with their children (6:1–4). Slaves are to obey their masters and live as if they are serving Christ. Slavery was a large part of society, and Paul was a member of a minority movement. He wrote to people in bad situations, instructing them how to live in a fallen creation. Masters likewise are to treat slaves kindly, knowing they too sit under a master (6:5–9). Some of these commands are standard. But Paul also speaks subversively. He addresses the marginalized groups first, gives them ethical volition, and cuts the husbands and masters down to size.

Warfare (6:10–24) / Ephesians appropriately ends with the battle between heaven and earth. The two realms overlap. Paul commands those in Ephesus to stand in warfare (6:10–20). Their fight is not against humans, but against the supernatural dark powers. They are therefore to stand and resist the dark powers. They stand not in their own strength but in the strength of the Lord (6:10–12). He is their Warrior. He is their conquering King. They put on His armor, and this means having faith, righteousness, peace, the Word of God, and looking toward their present and future salvation with prayer (6:13–20). Paul closes telling them he is sending another ambassador for their encouragement (6:21–24). A cosmic drama is unfolding. Their continual decision is whether they will live in the light or in darkness.

PHILIPPIANS

JOYFUL KINGDOM CITIZENS

The city of man and the city of God
are overlapping spheres.

But the city of God is now invading the city of man through the gospel. Philippi was a Roman colony with many retired Roman soldiers. Paul encourages a different sort of citizenship. Humility, joy, and service mark God's people who worship the true King, not self-service, disunity, and grumbling. This is all based on the "mind of Christ" found in the Christ hymn. Philippians is the most upbeat letter of Paul. It is laced with happy, confident, and supportive passages, even in the midst of dire circumstances. Paul's joy overflows as he thanks those in Philippi for their partnership in the advance of the gospel. He encourages them to live as joyful citizens of God's kingdom.

Paul urges a new way of inhabiting the city of man through examples of joyful humility. He begins with his own situation. His imprisonment has served to advance the gospel, and in this he rejoices (1:1–26). He calls them to also live as kingdom citizens (1:27–2:4), using Jesus as the ultimate example in the Christ hymn (2:5–18). Then he turns to Timothy and Epaphroditus, who also gave up comforts for the gospel (2:19–30), and concludes with warnings against false teachers contrasted with his own example of service and sacrifice (3:1–4:1). Finally, he exhorts them to unity and speaks of the fellowship they have in Christ (4:2–23). Humility, joy, and unity are marks of kingdom citizens.

PHILIPPIANS / JOYFUL KINGDOM CITIZENS

Gospel Advance 1:1–26

Despite Paul's chains, the gospel continues to spread.

Kingdom Citizens 1:27–30

Paul urges them to live out their heavenly citizenship in humility.

Joy in Unity 2:1–4

He calls them to humble unity based on their experience of God.

Christ's Humility 2:5–8

Jesus is the ultimate example of self-sacrificial service.

Christ's Exaltation 2:9–11

Because of His humility, Christ received the throne.

Imitate Christ 2:12–18

They need to work out their salvation, looking to Christ.

Examples 2:19–30

Timothy and Epaphroditus had the mind of Christ.

Paul's Example 3:1–4:1

Unlike the Judaizers, Paul presses on toward Jesus.

Joyful Peace 4:2–23

Paul exhorts the Philippians to follow Christlike examples.

Gospel Advance (1:1–26) / Paul begins by identifying himself as a servant of Christ Jesus, already hitting on one of his main themes: humility. He thanks God for those in Philippi because they have collaborated with him in the gospel. They have been generous and faithful to Paul through the gift from Epaphroditus. Since they began in this way, God will make sure they stay faithful. He also prays for them that they would be a more loving community and they would be able to discern the marks of the kingdom of God (1:3–11). Then he transitions to his own situation as an example of a new citizenship filled with humility and joy despite circumstances. His Roman imprisonment has actually led to more hearing the gospel, and he has joy despite his imprisonment. Rome doesn't run the show; God does. Paul is confident that he will be released since more ministry awaits, but he does not fear death. For he knows that either way he will be with Christ. His heavenly citizenship determines his earthly conduct (1:12–26).

Kingdom Citizens (1:27–30) / Paul then turns from his own circumstances to the Philippians, telling them to follow Christ's example and to live as worthy kingdom citizens (1:27). They are not to follow the ways of Rome. They have a new Savior. The purpose of this new citizenship is to stand firm in unity. A unified people is a strong, successful, and conquering people. They are to have one spirit and mind as they strive together toward their new home. They need this encouragement because the Philippians have opponents. Who these opponents are is unclear. It could be people outside the church like those who imprison Paul. But it could also be insiders, Judaizers who require circumcision and restrict their freedom (3:2–6) or those who emphasize freedom too much (3:18–21). No matter who it is, Paul says their end is destruction, but those in Philippi are destined for salvation. The congregation in Philippi will suffer under these opponents, but that is what it means to be part of this new heavenly city. They need to follow the virtuous examples around them, especially Christ Himself.

Joy in Unity (2:1–4) / Paul now expands on what this shared life looks like: one spirit and mind. A heavenly citizen is a united citizen, and a united people are a resilient people. He calls them to unity in the Spirit based on the shared experience of the triune God. God is the one who creates and sustains their harmony. In the midst of suffering they have encouragement in Christ, comfort in His love, participation in the Spirit. They have treasures in the Godhead. In light of these gifts, they are to complete Paul's joy by being cohesive: having the same mind and love. They are to do nothing for themselves but should count others as more significant than themselves. Paul has already embodied this in his own ministry. Now he will look to the ultimate example of sharing in the triune God's life with all humility and joy.

Christ's Humility (2:5–8) / This leads Paul into the great poem of Philippians. Paul has been speaking of the humility they need to embody; now he arrives at the paradigm for genuine spiritual progress. The prime exemplar of a heavenly citizen is Christ Himself. His self-sacrificial service stands above all others. In the Christ hymn (2:5–11), Paul traces Christ's journey from preexistence with God to His incarnation, death, resurrection, and ascension to the right hand of God. The text is full of allusions to Genesis 1–3 and Isaiah 52–53. He begins with Christ's humiliation. Jesus went from being in the form of God, to a servant (human being), to the cross, to death. He went down, down, down. Jesus did not selfishly exploit equality with God but put on human form. Christ emptied Himself by taking on human flesh and went all the way down to the most humiliating form of death: the cross. Jesus is the ultimate example of service.

Christ's Exaltation (2:9–11) / Because Jesus acted as Isaiah's Suffering Servant in contrast to the hubris of Adam, God exalted Him. Adam disobeyed and tried to grasp equality with God and was punished. Jesus acted as the new Adam, who did not take the fruit in the garden. He submitted His will to the Father and was rewarded. God exalted Jesus because of His humility and gave Him the sovereign name of Lord as the God-man (Isa. 52:13). He has now gone up, up, up. The purpose of this glorification is so that everyone might worship Him. Every knee will bow in the cosmos to the one Lord of all (Isa. 45:23). Every tongue will confess His sovereignty and power so that the Father might be glorified. If those in Philippi follow Christ's example, they too will be rewarded. Christ is their heavenly paradigm for earthly living. He is their Lord; they are His citizens.

Imitate Christ (2:12–18) / Paul then calls those in Philippi to imitate Christ's humble lifestyle. He tells them to work out their kingdom citizenship. They will not drift toward it; they need to work at it, for it won't be easy. And they need to do so with fear and trembling because they stand before their sovereign king (Ps. 2:11). If they feel like giving up, Paul reminds them it is ultimately God who works in them. Their perseverance is not suspended because God works in them; it is energized. They are not to be like the wandering Israelites who grumbled and complained as they sought a new land. They are to hold fast to Christ and keep running the race. Paul is in prison for their faith, but he is glad as long as they keep going. They shouldn't despair because of circumstances. Circumstances pale in light of their heavenly citizenship.

Examples (2:19–30) / Two coworkers who had the mind of Christ are now highlighted. Timothy genuinely cares for others, having the mindset of Christ Jesus. Paul has already instructed them to value others above themselves (2:3). Now Timothy stands as an embodied example. He has proven his worth in serving Paul as a son. Paul wishes to send him to Philippi before he comes. Timothy walks in Jesus' wake. Paul will also send back Epaphroditus with this letter. The Philippians had sent Epaphroditus to bring a financial gift to Paul. Like Timothy, Epaphroditus is a model of sacrificial gospel work. In fact, he grew so sick on this mission that he almost died. Like Christ, Epaphroditus was willing to give up his life for others. Both Timothy and Epaphroditus stand as examples of what it looks like to imitate Christ in His humility.

Paul's Example (3:1–4:1) / Timothy and Epaphroditus, who had the mind of Christ, are now contrasted to the Judaizers. The opponents are enemies of the cross who try to get Gentiles to follow the Jewish traditions. They are not laying down their life in humility for the joy of those in Philippi. Instead, they require more of them. The opponents boast in their Jewish pedigree and do not follow the example of Jesus, who did not exploit His privileges. But if anyone could boast in the flesh, it was Paul. He was a Jew with an impeccable history and résumé (3:1–6). However, like Christ, he gave them up. He considered all of these things as nothing compared to participating in suffering and sacrificial love. It was all rubbish to him. He gave it all up so that he might gain Christ and have Christ's righteousness. He understands that if he knows Christ's suffering, he will also know Christ's resurrection. So he presses on as a runner who races for the prize of a new kingdom (3:7–14). Paul therefore calls those in Philippi to imitate him and not the enemies of the cross. Their citizenship is in heaven and one day Christ will reward them (3:20).

Joyful Peace (4:2–23) / Paul finally exhorts the Philippian assembly toward unity and joy. He addresses two prominent women in the church, Euodia and Syntyche, to be of the same mind, language he has already used in 2:2. They are in some sort of conflict and need to follow Christ's example. He commands all the Philippians to rejoice and not be anxious about any pressures that face them but to bathe everything in prayer. God's peace will come to them no matter what the circumstance (4:4–7). He then urges them to think on what is virtuous and to follow the examples he has written about, including his own. He has learned to be content in whatever circumstance because God gives him strength in his weakness. Yet he is thankful that those in Philippi shared in his troubles and provided for him financially. He has received the gifts from Epaphroditus that they sent. They too have enacted Christ's model. Paul urges them to continue in the good that God has begun in them. Even those of Caesar's household greet those in Philippi. The city of God has come to the city of man.

COLOSSIANS

CHRIST IS ALL

The temptation is to add something to Christ.

To worship other things. To require certain rules. In Colossians, Paul argues Christ is all. He is preeminent. The church was tempted to worship angels or other spiritual beings and keep Jewish food laws and festivals. But Paul contends that Christ is all in all; He is the head of creation and the new creation. He has conquered the cosmic forces of darkness and all earthly principles, rules, and regulations. People can walk in Him as the new humanity. The vision is vast. The claim is mind-blowing. Christ is the key, the supreme Lord of heaven and earth.

Paul did not start the Colossian church, nor did he likely ever visit it, yet he writes to them arguing that Christ is all in light of the growing influence of pagan philosophies and Jewish legalism. He begins with the Colossians' faith but moves quickly to argue that Christ is preeminent over all creation (1:1–23). Paul's ministry is one of service and suffering on behalf of increased knowledge of Christ's sufficiency (1:24–2:7). In the second half he directly attacks the false teaching, asserting that they need to be built on Christ. The false philosophies are empty and can't deal with sin. They need to look to Christ, who is in heaven. For only Jesus has done what is necessary for new creation life (2:8–4:18).

COLOSSIANS / CHRIST IS ALL

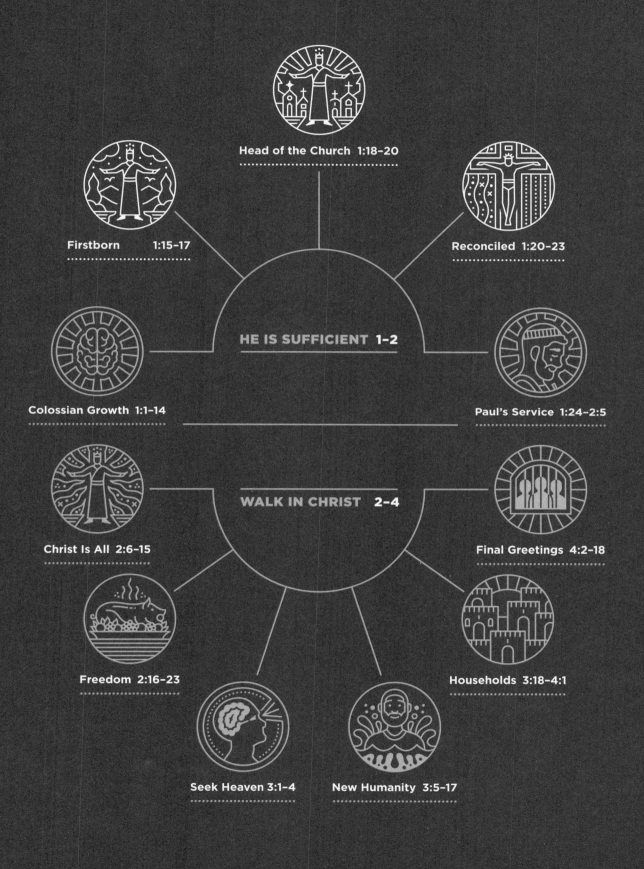

Head of the Church 1:18–20

Firstborn 1:15–17

Reconciled 1:20–23

HE IS SUFFICIENT 1–2

Colossian Growth 1:1–14

Paul's Service 1:24–2:5

WALK IN CHRIST 2–4

Christ Is All 2:6–15

Final Greetings 4:2–18

Freedom 2:16–23

Households 3:18–4:1

Seek Heaven 3:1–4

New Humanity 3:5–17

Colossian Growth (1:1–14) / Paul begins by thanking God for the Colossians' faith and prays that they would be filled with knowledge (1:3–8). They have trusted Jesus and love God's people. But Epaphras has also reported how they need perseverance and instruction in light of the false teaching. So Paul prays for a filling of knowledge, wisdom, and understanding (1:9–14). These themes of knowledge and wisdom become important in light of the emerging heresy. They need the true philosophy of Christ. They need increased knowledge of Christ so they can continue in the faith. They are no longer under the forces of darkness. In fact, they have been qualified to inherit the rights and privileges of angelic beings (saints in light). They shouldn't worship angels; they will stand above angels.

Firstborn (1:15–17) / The central theological argument is found in the Christ hymn, where Paul will source the rest of his admonitions. He argues that Jesus is the head of all things (1:15–20) but begins with His supremacy over creation. Verses 15–17 are a Christological reinterpretation of Genesis 1–2 and Proverbs 8:22. Jesus is God's Word, wisdom, and new humanity. He is the new Adam, the true image of the invisible God (Heb. 1:3). The Son stands above the cosmological order because He is the firstborn of creation. This does not mean He was the first created being; rather, He is the true heir and of special status and higher rank than any other. He also is the one through whom all things were created, even the angelic forces. In fact, all of these were created by Him and for Him. All of creation is under His authority. All of creation holds together in Him. Creation was through Him, to Him, and for Him. Nothing in all creation stands above Him. Christ is all.

Head of the Church (1:18–20) / Not only is Jesus the authority over creation, but He is the head of the new creation. God is reconciling the universe to Himself through Christ. Jesus is supreme Lord over the church. Jesus is the firstborn of creation, but He is also the firstborn from the dead. Salvation was not a release from embodied realities but a redeeming of them. The new creation project begins with Christ and flows to the church. Paul says it begins with Christ for two reasons. First, so that He might be preeminent, which means in the first place, or above all. Second, Jesus uniquely redeems because He is fully divine. The fullness of God dwells in Him. God's word, wisdom, glory, and power reside in the Messiah. If Jesus was the main agent in creation, then He is also God's main agent in reconciliation. The mechanism for this reconciling work was His blood on the cross; blood unites what was broken at the fall.

Reconciled (1:20–23) / The cross reconciles not only people but also the whole universe. Blood heals. Blood brings peace. Jesus' blood is the hinge on which the universe turns. Those in Colossae were once opposed to Christ in their minds. They were separated from the work of the Son. But now through Jesus' bodily death they have been brought together. The purpose of welcoming them was to make them set apart as His own people. Jesus' work made them whole and clean before Him, ready for the new era. However, they are not there yet. They have need for perseverance. They need to press on in the faith, not putting anything in heaven or on earth above Christ. The supremacy, preeminence, and authority of Christ is Paul's message, and the Colossians must cling to it and not be tempted by other philosophies that distract them from Jesus and His work.

Paul's Service (1:24–2:5) / Paul turns to his own ministry, focusing on his suffering and stewardship in the context of Christ's cosmic work. Paul is in prison, and it is through Paul's suffering that he manifests and reveals the mystery of Christ. Christ's suffering brings reconciliation, and Paul is also a reconciling agent who suffers like Christ. He therefore rejoices in his suffering. For his suffering reveals and encourages the church that the old world is ending and the new world is beginning (1:24). Paul is also a steward of God. He reveals the mystery of Christ: Gentiles as fellow inheritors of God's promise. The "mystery" is not made known through other philosophies but in Christ alone (1:25–27). He discloses this mystery to all churches so that they might continue in obedience (1:28–2:3). In fact, Paul's suffering should spur their obedience and understanding of the mystery that is Christ. In Christ "are hidden all the treasures of wisdom and knowledge" (2:3). Paul reminds them of his message and service to them so that they might not be tempted by vain philosophies (2:4–7).

Christ Is All (2:6–15) / Paul now attacks the emerging philosophy head on in 2:8–4:18. The Colossians need to recognize that Christ is all. They were tempted to believe Jesus was just another spiritual being alongside others and that they needed to follow certain Jewish traditions. He refutes the false teaching point by point. He contrasts the emptiness of philosophy, human tradition, and the elemental forces with the fullness of the Messiah. Paul urges them not to be taken captive by other teachings (2:8). The false philosophy is according to human tradition, which were probably Jewish expansions of the Torah. He also identifies the heresy with the elemental forces, probably hostile cosmic powers of the universe. These teachings are not according to Jesus. Christ is above these teachings in various ways (2:9–15). First, Jesus is the embodiment of the divine. Second, the Colossians have been filled with Christ and therefore filled with the divine. If so, then they have conquered the hostile cosmic powers since Christ has conquered them. Third, in Jesus they have been marked out as the people of God through both spiritual circumcision and baptism. God has made them alive by reconciling them through the cross and disarming all cosmic powers. How can they turn to these philosophies when the fullness of Christ resides in them?

Freedom (2:16–23) / Paul turns to the implications of Christ's supremacy. If Christ's work is superior to the cosmic powers and even Jewish traditions, then they shouldn't let anyone condemn them for Jewish practices such as food, drink, or the celebration of certain days. Nor should anyone require asceticism, worship of angels, or visions. They are free in Christ. These things are a shadow, but He is the substance. Jesus is the Head, and the whole church is built up through Him, not these practices, into a temple of God. He is all they need. In Him they have died to the cosmic powers. Therefore how can they submit to regulations such as "Do not handle, Do not taste, Do not touch"? Abstinence, separation, and purity in this case are human teachings and only have the outward appearance of religion; they don't stop sin in the flesh. The other philosophies don't deliver on what they promise, so now Paul will turn to living out the new creation through Christ.

Seek Heaven (3:1–4) / Rather than focusing their attention on these worldly commands, Paul encourages the Colossians to seek the things above where Christ is seated. The things above refer to Christ's sufficiency and reign over the cosmos. The Colossians are even seated with Him; union with Christ and His supremacy is the main antidote to false teaching. Paul reminds them that this is not merely a theological claim, but they are truly united to Christ in their baptism. They have died with Christ and their life is hidden with Christ, and therefore they are one with Him. They need not be distracted by this false teaching and these earthly commands, for when Jesus appears they will have their reward. Christ has already conquered and been raised up, but they also await the day when His glory will be more fully manifested and revealed upon the earth.

New Humanity (3:5–17) / Paul contrasts the way of heaven with the way of the earth, the new humanity with the old humanity. Freedom in Christ does not mean freedom from any moral obligation. The mystery of union with Christ transforms their lives on the earth as they wait for their inheritance. He tells them to put to death earthly things: sexual immorality, covetousness, anger, slander, obscene talk, and lying. They used to walk in these ways, but now their life is hidden with Christ in heaven. He uses baptismal and clothing imagery of putting off and putting on. They have put on the new humanity and put off the old humanity, so how can they turn back to rules and regulations? New image bearers of God are being made after the image of Christ, their Head. In the church, it doesn't matter if one is educated or uneducated, rich or poor, Jew or Greek. Christ is all they need.

As the new Adam, He calls them to put on compassion, kindness, patience, and above all love, which is the bond of wholeness. Christ exemplified these, and now they can walk in them.

Households (3:18–4:1) / Paul applies Christ's triumph and the reality of the new humanity—the true philosophy—to the first-century Roman family: households. The new humanity is lived out in husbands and wives, masters and slaves, and parents and children. Some of these commands are standard. But Paul also speaks subversively. He addresses the marginalized groups first, gives them ethical volition, and cuts the "masters" down to size. He also based all of these commands on their relationship to the true Lord of the universe. Wives are to submit to their husbands, and husbands are to love their wives. Children are to obey parents, for this pleases Jesus. Fathers are to not provoke their children. Slaves are to obey their masters and live as if they are serving Christ. Christ will reward those who do good when He returns. Masters likewise are to treat slaves kindly, knowing they too sit under a master in heaven. Paul does not abolish structures of obedience; he presses into them because of Christ's supremacy.

Final Greetings (4:2–18) / Paul closes his letter with final exhortations, a commendation of his coworkers, and concluding greetings. The themes of the letter are also present: Paul speaks of the spread of the gospel, his sufferings in prison, the mystery of Christ, and the quality of Epaphras's ministry. Essentially, he solidifies his relationship with Colossae, urging them to heed his warnings. The new philosophy posed a risk to Colossae. Paul gives his final greetings, showing they are friends in the gospel, even though he had likely never been to their city. They must believe that the Messiah is the key to the universe. False philosophies are from the earth. Christ is all.

1 THESSALONIANS

HOLINESS & HOPE

Since humans began telling stories,
they've been envisioning the end.

How will it come about, who will survive, and what will happen afterward? What people think about the end reveals what they believe about ultimate reality. A culture's ultimate hopes and fears are uncovered by their view of the apocalypse. Paul argues in 1 Thessalonians that the future return of Christ governs how to inhabit the world as citizens of the kingdom. There is hope, despite the pain.

In 1 Thessalonians, Paul argues that Christ's return should compel holiness and hope in the midst of hardship. This is a suffering community, but in every chapter Paul draws their attention to the return of Christ and the comfort it will convey. He devotes a large section of his letter to this theme (4:13–5:11). However, the imminent return of the King must also inspire holiness. Eschatology determines ethics. Paul encourages them by not only speaking about the return of Christ but also by recounting his own ministry among them (1–3). Chapters 1–3 therefore assure the suffering community about the reality of their faith, while chapters 4–5 instruct them to put their faith into practice.

1 THESSALONIANS / HOLINESS & HOPE

THANKSGIVING   1:1–10

Paul's thanksgiving for their faith.

MINISTRY   2–3

Paul's gospel ministry both in his presence and absence.

Paul's Presence 2:1–12

He preached, worked hard, and loved them.

Thanksgiving 2:13–16

He is thankful for their response despite affliction.

Paul's Absence 2:17–3:10

He tried to come to them, but sent Timothy.

PRAYER   3:11–13

That their hearts would be blameless at Jesus' return.

INSTRUCTIONS   4–5

That they would live a life that pleases God in holiness.

Holiness   4:1–12

Be holy, sexually pure, hard-working, and loving.

Hope   4:13–5:11

Christ is returning; the dead and alive will meet Him.

Community 5:12–22

Be at peace with each other and with God.

BENEDICTION 5:23–28

God will make them holy at the second coming of Christ.

THANKSGIVING (1:1–10)

The thanksgiving (1:2–10), prayer (3:11–13), and benediction (5:23–24) are shorthand summaries of Paul's concerns in the letter, yet each of them escalates in hope. In all these he encourages them toward a holy life in light of Jesus' return. The thanksgiving focuses on the Thessalonians' authentic response to the gospel when Paul visited them (Acts 17:1–9). They exhibited faith, love, and hope. The gospel came in power, and they became imitators of Jesus in their suffering. Their example under persecution has sounded forth to the whole region. It is clear that the context of the letter is suffering. Paul speaks of their severe suffering and concludes with a word about Christ's return. They wait for Jesus, who will deliver them from the wrath to come. Though the present reality is difficult, a happy hope is on the horizon.

MINISTRY (2–3)

In chapters 2–3, Paul recounts his authentic gospel ministry, covering both the nature of his past presence (2:1–12) and defending his current absence (2:17–3:10), with another thanksgiving in the middle (2:13–16). Paul assures them of his faithfulness concerning his two major responsibilities: the Word of God and the people of God. Paul was above reproach as a steward and herald of the Word. He was also caring and exemplary in his relationship to the people (2:1–12). Now that he has left them, he longs to encourage them because of their affliction, but he could not come to them. So he sent Timothy, who has reported to him their faith and love in spite of hardship.

Paul's Presence (2:1–12) / Paul reminds the Thessalonians that while he was with them, he was a faithful minister. He was an ambassador in regard to the Word of God (2:1–6). His method was pure, he did not come with a greedy heart or seeking glory from others, and he told them the truth. He was also faithful as a minister to the people of God. He acted like a mother with them, in that he cared intimately for them (2:7–8). He worked hard among them, laboring at tentmaking so as not to charge them (2:9–10). Finally, he was a father who exhorted them (2:11–12). If they had any reason to doubt his motives, his hard work, directness, and lack of greed display his pure intentions. If they have any reason to doubt their faith, it is not on account of his ministry. Paul gives his own example to encourage them in their faith and call them to imitation in the midst of suffering.

Thanksgiving (2:13–16) / Paul continues to thank God for this suffering but stable community. They received the Word, applied the Word, and displayed the Word. Paul thanks God for similar things he mentioned in 1:2–10, but he adds key elements. He sets his gaze on their suffering, identifying the Jews and Gentiles as the source. Paul recounts the historical pattern of Jewish rejection of the gospel and their active persecution, tracing it back to their rejection of Jesus, the prophets, and Paul. Though Paul speaks in this way about Jews, this is not directed at all Jews, as Paul himself is a Jew. He writes as a member of a minority movement, and his purpose is to encourage the Thessalonians and assure them about the reality of their faith. Even though they are under attack, justice will come to their persecutors.

Paul's Absence (2:17–3:10) / Paul shifts from his presence to his absence, maybe subtly alluding to the theme of Jesus' future presence and current absence, which envelops the letter. Paul affirms his love for the Thessalonians and defends his absence. His heart is on full display. In 2:17–20, he explains his current absence. His great desire is to be with them, but Satan has hindered his return. They may have been upset that Paul left while they suffered. In 3:1–5, Paul then explains that his love for them caused him to send Timothy to see how they were doing in the midst of persecution. He hopes Timothy's presence will encourage them to stand fast, for suffering will come to them all. He is afraid Satan might have derailed some of them. Timothy returns and gives an encouraging report (3:6–10). They long to see Paul, and Paul is comforted about their progress.

PRAYER (3:11–13)

At the center of the letter is a prayer that points both backward to what Paul has covered and forward to the second half—functioning as a hinge to the entire letter. The first request is that the Lord might allow Paul to come to them (2:17–18; 3:6, 10). The second request is that their love grow for one another. The love that the Thessalonians have for one another has already been noted (1:3; 3:6) and will continue to be encouraged (4:9–12). His prayer concludes by drawing their eyes to the coming of Christ. Paul's final and climactic entreaty is that believers be established so that they might be blameless in holiness at the coming of Jesus. This is a summary of Paul's concern for the letter as a whole. Paul sees eschatology and ethics as interwoven. Eschatology is the basis for their holiness. He has seen holiness (1:1–10), he prays for more (3:11–13), and God will make it happen (5:23–24).

INSTRUCTIONS (4–5)

Paul desires to complete the things lacking in the Thessalonians' faith. He has heard of their faith and love, but they need more hope. In this second part of the letter, he instructs them about their behavior, hope, and life in the community. Regarding their behavior, he focuses especially on sexual self-control and brotherly love (4:1–12). Then he provides more details on Christ's return, giving comfort concerning the dead in Christ (4:13–18) and the living (5:1–11). Finally, Paul provides a smattering of commands concerning worship in the church (5:12–22). They are to be at peace with one another and with God while they stand up under the gaze of a hostile world.

Holiness (4:1–12) / Paul begins the second half of the letter with his thesis: God's will for their life is holiness. They need to become a distinct people in light of Christ's return. He immediately applies this to sexuality (4:1–8). Gentiles in the congregation would have found it hard to change their practices. He wants them to separate from sexual immorality, learn to control themselves, and not harm others in this. These commands are based on three foundations: the future judgment of the Lord, the past call of God, and the present gift of the Holy Spirit. Then he turns to brotherly love and daily work (4:9–12). He encourages them, saying he has already seen their love, but he wants it to increase. In fact, he wants them to love, live quietly, mind their own business, and work. They need to be good citizens in light of their suffering and give no one reason for persecution.

Hope (4:13–5:11) / Paul now comforts them concerning the dead (4:13–18) and the living (5:1–11). Possibly those who died are martyrs in the community, and people wondered what happened to the dead. Details about Christ's return provide the foundation for this consolation. First, he answers what will happen to the dead in Christ at His return. The dead will have priority at Christ's return. Jesus' return is explained as a triumphal return of a ruler to His city. The people of the city would go out to meet the king, welcoming Him into His kingdom. The Lord descends from heaven, then the dead in Christ rise *first*. Those who are still alive will follow, being caught up with the dead in the air to meet the Lord. After the procession, all will be with the Lord forever. For believers, the final day is to be not one of apprehension but of anticipation, not of panic but of peace, not of rumor but of realism. In chapter 5, Paul turns to comfort those still alive. He says Christ's return will mean destruction for their enemies (5:1–3) but hope and comfort for them (5:4–10). When those who oppose them claim "peace and security," judgment will come. Rome promised them peace and safety under the *Pax Romana*, but that will be reversed at Christ's return. The Thessalonians are sons of light. They are to be awake and ready for Jesus' return. This is all for their comfort.

Community (5:12–22) / Paul concludes by addressing fellowship and worship in the church. The pressures on the outside create the need for peace internally. First, he tells them to respect and honor their leaders (5:12–13). Then he instructs them how to act with various members of the community who are struggling: the idle, the fainthearted, and the weak. They are to be patient with them all (5:14). He also commands them, like Jesus did, to not respond to evil with evil. Outsiders might attack them but they are to respond in love (5:15). Finally, he speaks about their attitude and actions toward God (5:16–18). They are to rejoice even in the midst of persecution, pray always, and give thanks in all circumstances. They are not to quench the Spirit nor despise prophecies. Ultimately the community is to be a place of peace and joy in a hostile world.

BENEDICTION (5:23–28)

Paul concludes the letter with a benediction, bringing his entire letter to a conclusion. He returns to and completes the themes found in the thanksgiving and prayer. He prays that the God of peace will sanctify the Thessalonians completely at the coming of Jesus. Emphasizing God's peace counters the *Pax Romana* and also indicates God's plan is to bring peace to His people at the Son's return. They are to be holy in the meantime. Blamelessness at the return of the King is the theme for the letter. Although the letter has been filled with encouragement and commands, Paul concludes saying God will do it! He will make them holy. What Paul has prayed, God will accomplish by His sovereign will.

2 THESSALONIANS

STAND FIRM

Wait. Be patient. Be faithful.

That is the call of Christians as they anticipate Jesus' return. In the meantime, there will be persecution and temptations to get off track. In the end, God will balance the justice tables; He will put everything right. The Thessalonians were tempted to think they had been forgotten and Jesus had already returned. They thought their persecution revealed they were not the people of God, but the opposite was the case. It revealed they were worthy. It revealed they would be vindicated on the last day. Paul encourages them to continue to stand firm as they loyally wait for Jesus' return.

Paul writes to the Thessalonian church, rebutting claims that the day of the Lord has already come; he writes to correct and comfort. He does so by giving them encouragement in their persecution. He speaks of God's judgment on their enemies (1), corrects their timeline of the final day (2), and exhorts them to continue doing good and avoid those who are idle (3). They need to stand firm in the midst of confusion and maltreatment, faithfully waiting for Jesus' just return. The reigning King will set things right on the last day, and they are to be ready.

2 THESSALONIANS / STAND FIRM

ENCOURAGEMENT 1

Paul reassures them by considering Christ's fiery return.

Commendation 1:3–4

He thanks God for their fortitude in persecution.

Comfort 1:5–10

Christ's punishment of the unbelievers is a comfort.

Worthy 1:11–12

He prays that they would be made worthy of God's calling.

ENLIGHTENMENT 2

Paul adjusts their last-day theology, speaking of Christ's return.

Rebellion 2:1–12

The rebellion and lawless man must come first.

Stand Firm 2:13–15

Stand firm in persecution because of Christ's return.

Hope 2:16–17

He prays they might have hope and comfort in suffering.

EXHORTATION 3

Paul asks for prayer and insists that the idle keep working.

Deliverance 3:1–5

He prays that God's Word might speed ahead.

Idleness 3:6–15

The idle must work and the rest are to avoid them.

Peace 3:16–18

He prays that the God of peace might give them peace.

ENCOURAGEMENT (1)

Paul begins by giving encouragement to the suffering Thessalonian church. Like the previous letter, the context of 2 Thessalonians is a mistreated and confused church. He thanks God for their faith and steadfastness in the midst of persecution. They participate in God's kingdom by waiting for Jesus' return. Persecution does not disqualify them; it qualifies them. When Jesus comes, He will judge those who oppose His people with fire. God will rebalance the world at the right time. Paul prays that the church would be made worthy of God's kingdom through their time of testing.

Commendation (1:3–4) / Paul is thankful for the Thessalonians. They have shown evidence of an active faith and love, two of the cardinal Christian virtues. And they have done this while being mistreated. Paul even boasts about the Thessalonians because he knows about their endurance in the midst of suffering. They suffer well, following their Savior who also suffered unjustly. Yet they also need to have hope. They are confused about the return of Jesus and may begin to falter.

Comfort (1:5–10) / Paul not only praises their endurance but comforts them concerning their afflictions. He does so by speaking of the justice of God. When Jesus returns, He will bring the fire to those who persecute them. Essentially, this is a defense of God's goodness as some may have been questioning God in light of their circumstances. However, Jesus will repay the adversaries for what they have done to God's people, and the opponents will experience separation from their Creator. This is eschatological reversal. On that day, Jesus will be honored among His people as He comes to rescue them and bring them rest. Though the time is not here yet, it is coming.

Worthy (1:11–12) / At the end of every chapter, Paul prays for the Thessalonians. Here he prays that they would be made worthy of God's calling. He doesn't want persecution to knock them off track. The oppression is their time of testing, like it was for Israel and Jesus. It is through this mistreatment they are made pure for God's kingdom. Their suffering is not their shame; it makes them worthy of the kingdom. Their mistreatment doesn't make them outsiders; it makes them commendable. They need to press on in good works. Paul is not only thankful for them, and comforts them, but prays that they might continue in steadfastness as they stand firm in the hope of Jesus' second coming.

ENLIGHTENMENT (2)

The Thessalonians feared they may have missed or been forgotten at Jesus' second coming. Paul tells them certain events must come first and comforts them. Jesus' powerful breath will end it all. The rebellion and man of lawlessness must precede Jesus' return. The lawless one will deceive many with the power of Satan, but the church must stand firm. The ultimate revelation of this "antichrist" has not been manifested, but his work is already evident. However, like their opponents, the lawless one will be killed by a breath from the Lord. The Thessalonians' future is sure and secure. They need to endure while they wait.

Rebellion (2:1–12) / Paul corrects their last-day theology, again providing comfort for those waiting for Jesus. They thought the day of the Lord had already come (2:1–2). But that day can't come until the rebellion and the man of lawlessness arrive (2:3–10). The lawless person (the name comes from Daniel 11:36–37 and Ezek. 28:2–10) follows in the footsteps of Nebuchadnezzar, Antiochus IV Epiphanes, Herod Agrippa, and General Pompey. This figure will persecute God's people and require worship. Though these things are already at work and many believe the lie, a final climactic manifestation will occur. A certain "restrainer" (likely the archangel Michael or the Holy Spirit) is holding him back in the meantime (see 2:6–7). When the lawless one comes to persecute God's people with the power of Satan, the breath of Jesus will kill him once and for all. It won't even be a battle. The Sovereign will wield His power in a climactic act.

Stand Firm (2:13–15) / Because "the rebellion" is already at work and to be more fully manifested in the future, God's people need to stand firm. They stand in the midst of a storm. They need to plant their feet resolutely on solid rock. Paul contrasts the destruction of the wicked with those loved by God. The church is God's firstfruits. They know from Paul's teaching the end of those who oppose God. God's opponents will be destroyed when Jesus returns. But the Thessalonians are God's chosen people and will be saved. They will obtain glory while the rest receive fire. Therefore, they need to persevere and hold fast to Jesus and Paul's teachings. The last day will overturn all injustices with the arrival of the Just One.

Hope (2:16–17) / Again, Paul closes the chapter with a prayer. He writes these things not to scare them or cause them to tremble but to give comfort. Their future is sure. The rebellious will face judgment away from God's presence. Jesus came to give them "eternal comfort and good hope" (2:16). Paul prays that this would be true as they remember that God is for them. Their enemies will suffer punishment from God if they don't turn from their ways. The Thessalonians can rest in hope.

EXHORTATION (3)

The heavenly battle described in chapter 2 is not divorced from the earthly realm. Paul has chronicled the coming of the lawless man and the restrainer, and these events have implications for their time in Thessalonica. Jesus' return activates and energizes good works. The destruction of the wicked compels confidence. The Thessalonians need to embody their hope and steadfastness in everyday life. Paul therefore requests protection for his own ministry, exhorts the church concerning the idle, and prays they would have peace.

Deliverance (3:1–5) / Part of the Thessalonians' steadfastness includes pleading to God concerning Paul's mission. Paul asks for prayer. Prayer that his message would speed ahead and that he would be rescued from the wicked. As the Thessalonians suffer, as the future will include a rebellion, so too Paul experiences opposition. Like Jesus, Paul carries a cross. But he does so in order that Jesus' name might be known. The Thessalonians must also pick up their crosses. So he asks for prayer. God can make a way. But Paul also urges them to put their trust in God. God will protect them and give them endurance.

Idleness (3:6–15) / Another application of steadfastness is avoiding those who are idle. Followers of Jesus should not be idle but imitate Jesus and Paul in working hard so that they might be able to provide for others. The reason for idleness is unknown. It could be that some were waiting for Jesus' return. More likely some in the congregation stopped working because wealthy members sustained them. Paul supports his command about idleness by reminding them of his own example and teaching (see chapter 2). They need to press on in doing good. If someone persists in idleness, the church needs to separate from them for their own good and the witness of the church. Waiting for Jesus means not only waiting, but active and energetic waiting.

Peace (3:16–18) / Paul closes with a third prayer. He has asked that they might be worthy of God's kingdom, that they would have hope, and now he requests peace. Though the Thessalonians are suffering, they worship the God of shalom. Paul prays that God would give them peace in this hard time. Rome will never give them the peace they desire. They need not fear, for God is for them. Though they may have received letters saying the day of the Lord has come, this is Paul's true letter, and they can trust it. He has instructed them on what is to come, and what to do while they patiently and faithfully wait.

1 TIMOTHY

GUARD
THE DEPOSIT

**False teaching can seep into a church
and eat away at the roots.**

No strength, depth, or vitality is left in a corrupted church. Destruction follows. Paul writes to Timothy, telling him to confront the false teaching in Ephesus. Positively, he instructs him how to act in God's household, which is the foundation for the truth. Military imagery pervades the letter. Timothy must wage the warfare, fight the good fight, and guard the deposit. The battle for God's people is war. Weapons must be taken up. Armor must be donned. The future of God's people is at stake.

Timothy was sent to Ephesus by Paul to put things in order, to confront false teaching, to guard the deposit entrusted to him. The nature of the false teaching is unclear, but it seemed to include both Jewish elements (1:6–11) and cultural influences (4:1). The letter begins and ends with Timothy's commission: wage the warfare (1) and guard the deposit (6). Between these panels are Paul's instructions for ordering the church (2–3), more details on the pressures that threaten the church, and Timothy's appropriate response (4–5). In sum, God's household is worth protecting. Timothy's task lies ahead of him.

1 TIMOTHY / GUARD THE DEPOSIT

COMMISSION 1

Timothy needs to wage warfare, protecting the deposit.

THE CHURCH 2–3

They will guard the deposit by living it out in the assembly.

THREATS 4–5

False teaching threatens to disrupt the church.

COMMISSION 6

Timothy should guard the deposit, eschewing false knowledge.

False Teaching 1:3–11

The false teachers spread myths and genealogies.

Prayer 2:1–7

They are to pray for all people so they might live quiet lives.

False Teaching 4:1–5

The error includes demonic teaching and asceticism.

Contentment 6:3–10

False teachers seek wealth, but contentment is Christ's way.

Grace 1:12–17

Despite his past, Paul was appointed by Jesus.

Men & Women 2:8–15

Men and women are to act appropriately in the church.

Good Servant 4:6–16

Timothy is to follow good doctrine and avoid myths.

Fight 6:11–16

Keep fighting the good fight and keep God's commands.

Warfare 1:18–20

Timothy is to fight against false teaching in Ephesus.

Leaders 3

Timothy is to appoint qualified overseers and deacons.

God's Household 5

The church is to honor true widows and elders.

Guard 6:17–21

Timothy is to guard the deposit entrusted to him.

COMMISSION (1)

Paul begins by giving Timothy his commission: wage the warfare, fight the good fight. In Ephesus, false teaching has crept into the church. Timothy must wage war on this new teaching and extinguish it before it devastates the church. The adversaries and their teaching results in lack of love, stumbling, and twists the purpose of the law. Though Paul also used to act in ignorance, God's grace alone separates Paul from the false teachers. Jesus came to save sinners; His message is for all. Some have rejected Paul's teaching; they have made a shipwreck of their faith. Timothy must fight; he must press on for the health of the church.

False Teaching (1:3–11) / Paul commands Timothy to confront the false teaching. This is Timothy's mission. Paul spends less time on the identity of the teachers or content of the aberration; his focus is on its effect, on the fruit it produces. However, in this section he does identify that the false teaching in Ephesus includes myths, genealogies, speculations, and vain discussions that push people off the path. These teachings do not promote love, trust in God's plan, or sincere faith. Though the law is good, these teachers corrupt the law by using it for their own purposes rather than its intended effect. It sounds as if they argue for some sort of genealogical superiority based on the Torah.

Grace (1:12–17) / In contrast to the false teaching, the true gospel produces faith, love, mercy, and acceptance. Paul is a prime example of this. God's grace alone separates Paul from the false teachers. Though Paul formerly fought against Jesus, he received mercy because Jesus came to save sinners. Jesus came offering salvation to all. The false teachers are focusing on genealogies, but the gospel is for everyone, even the worst of sinners. God is patient with people because He came to redeem the world. They should not listen to speculations about who God's people are or what they need to do. They worship Jesus. He offers them eternal life because He is the eternal King.

Warfare (1:18–20) / Timothy's commission was mentioned at the beginning of the chapter when he told him to combat false teaching (1:3), and now Paul returns to the command. He tells him to fight the good fight. Timothy must recall his past. It was to this task he was appointed. Prophecies were even made over him. Paul contrasts the fate of Hymenaeus and Alexander with Timothy. They have made a shipwreck of their faith, but Timothy needs to press on in faith with a good conscience. He will receive eternal life if he does. Timothy was sent to Ephesus to put things in order, and he must take up the sword of faith now to safeguard the church.

THE CHURCH (2-3)

In the middle of the letter, Paul turns to what it looks like to live faithfully in the church in contrast to the false teaching. He focuses on worship in the church and its leaders. The false teaching was already disturbing church practices, so he urges order and proper behavior in God's household. This includes prayer for the salvation of all people (2:1-7), proper conduct for men and women (2:8-15), and finally, establishing qualified leaders (3). Paul hopes to come to them soon but writes concerning conduct in God's household. The church is built on the person of Christ, and an orderly and true assembly is the best antidote to corruption (3:14-16).

Prayer (2:1-7) / After a short description of the false teaching and Timothy's commission in the first chapter, Paul turns to conduct in God's household, first addressing the topic of prayer. The speculations, myths, and genealogies likely had some impact on their prayer life. As Paul affirmed God's mercy for him despite his sin, he tells the congregation to pray for all people—even kings and those in authority. The church has a universal mission and God wants all people to be saved. God invites all people into His kingdom. Jesus is the Mediator for everyone who confesses His name. This is this message that Paul preaches. Timothy must now fight for it.

Men & Women (2:8-15) / The false teaching was also impacting how men and women acted in the church. A certain demeanor during public worship is called for because of the distinction between man and woman. The problem with men was their anger. Rather than quarreling, they were to raise their hands in prayer, asking the Lord of heaven and earth to answer their request (2:8). Paul spends more time on women than men here likely because the false teaching was particularly fruitful among women in this context (see 5:13-16; 2 Tim. 3:5-9). The problem with women was that they were dressing inappropriately and not evidencing proper submission (2:9-15). Women were not to draw attention to their wealth or availability but to their good works. They were to learn but not to teach or hold authority over men. Whether this was specific to the Ephesian context is debated, but the main idea is that men and women are to act properly in worship.

Leaders (3) / Not only does Timothy need to instruct those in Ephesus to pray and act according to their gender, but it is essential that he appoints qualified leaders who are able to teach and can contradict the false teaching. The list of qualifications for pastors stands in sharp contrast to the false teachers. Most of the credentials reflect outward observable behavior. The false teaching led to vices; true doctrine leads to virtue. The overseers must have a good family life, be devoted to their wives, gentle, able to teach, not greedy, and have a good reputation among those outside the church (3:1-7). Deacons, who are lead servants, must also walk in the truth (3:8–13). Paul closes this section with a summary. He reminds Timothy that his instructions should be put under the banner of how people ought to conduct themselves in God's house (3:14–16). Timothy's calling was to support, defend, and build up the church because it is in the church that the truth is seen.

THREATS (4–5)

Paul returns to the topic of false teaching in chapters 4 and 5 and contrasts the corruption with Timothy's proper service in God's church. While the false teachers follow the teaching of demons and forbid good things that God has given His people, Timothy is to have nothing to do with their myths but teach sound doctrine (4). Paul applies this teaching to various groups in the church (household codes) but focuses especially on widows who were spellbound by the false teaching. He tells Timothy to support true widows but be wary of those who have been seized by the myths (5:1–16). Again, the fruit of the false teaching rather than the content is emphasized. Paul closes the section speaking of honoring leaders in the congregation (5:17–18). If the false teaching is going to be dealt with, there needs to be trust between the leaders and the congregation.

False Teaching (4:1–5) / Paul supplements his description of the false teaching from chapter 1. This doctrine is sourced in demons and deceitful spirits. This should come as no surprise to Timothy. The Spirit predicted these things would happen. The errors of the teaching revolve around asceticism. They say marriage and food are to be shunned, which might be connected to a distortion of the law (see 1:7). Paul affirms that everything God created is good and is to be accepted with thanksgiving. The false teachers seek to restrict their freedom. Paul seeks to set them free.

Good Servant (4:6–16) / In contrast to the false teachers, Timothy's responsibility is to be a good servant of Jesus Christ. He is to feed on Christ, spread good teaching, and train for godliness. He is to have nothing to do with their silly myths and remember that this asceticism can have some value, but the pursuit of godliness is primary. Jesus has offered them eternal life. Why regulate what is to be done on the earth? Jesus is the Savior of all people, and the false teachers put up walls (4:6–10). A string of commands fill out the next section as Paul provides the paradigm of a healthy teacher (4:11–16). Timothy is to set an example for others in his conduct and perseverance. He is to function as a model for the congregation to follow.

God's Household (5) / How Timothy responds to various people in the congregation can also be a threat to the deposit. This section continues a previous theme. Timothy is to be a model of a healthy teacher, and this means knowing how to interact with various groups. The household codes in 1 Timothy are unique compared to other New Testament guidelines. The focus is more on how Timothy is to treat the congregation, and widows receive the majority of the attention. Paul begins with how to treat older men and women (5:1–2). The largest section deals with instructions about honoring widows (5:3–16). Paul tells him how to identify true widows, contrasts the activities of younger widows with real widows, and urges Timothy to honor true widows who need help. Some of these women were seduced by the false teaching, so Timothy must be careful here. Finally, Paul turns to instructions about elders (5:17–25). Though the subject changes, the theme of honor continues. The congregation is to honor elders by supporting them financially and respecting them.

COMMISSION (6)

In the final chapter, Paul returns to Timothy's commission. He repeats that Timothy is to confront false teaching (6:3) and tells Timothy to flee from the works of the flesh that follow in the train of this teaching and to pursue godliness (6:11). Timothy is to fight the good fight, relying on their Savior King. He is to guard what has been entrusted to him and avoid the false teaching. By doing this, he will save himself and his hearers. The false teachers are on the road to destruction, but God has offered eternal life in Jesus Christ.

Contentment (6:3–10) / Paul again urges Timothy to reject the false teaching that produces false fruit. The myths, genealogies, and speculations promote only quarreling, suspicion, and envy. This teaching is motivated by greed. Timothy's life is to be in contrast to these teachers. He is to have contentment and godliness. Those who wish to be rich fall into temptation and shipwreck their faith. Jesus taught on the danger of greed. Timothy is to show himself pure in this area. He is to pursue godliness rather than wealth.

Fight (6:11–16) / Paul recasts Timothy's commission, telling him to fight the good fight of faith. He is to pursue not wealth or fame, but godliness, faith, love, and gentleness. The genuine character of God's leaders in the church is set against the backdrop of the false teacher's greed. Timothy is to take hold of eternal life, which is offered in Jesus Christ, by rejecting this incipient heresy. The third poem of the letter is found in this section. All three of the poems speak about Jesus and His offer of eternal life (1:17; 3:16; 6:15–16). Jesus stands as the Savior and King of all. This confession is the foundation for Paul's commands and commission.

Guard (6:17–21) / In the last words of the letter, Paul does two things. He clarifies his perspective on wealth (6:17–19) and repeats his charge to Timothy to engage with the opponents (6:20–21). The rich in this age are not at fault for being rich. They should put their trust not in their riches but in God. They should be generous with what they have and store up treasures for themselves in heaven. Finally, Paul repeats and summarizes his commission to Timothy: guard the deposit. Timothy is to avoid the false teachers and protect what has been entrusted to him. The church is the foundation and pillar of the truth. Timothy must fight as a good soldier in God's army.

2 TIMOTHY

FAITHFUL
TO THE END

This is Paul's testament, his final letter
before he departs.

In it he encourages Timothy to persist in the midst of persecution, giving his own example and pointing Timothy to Christ. Though Paul's life has been filled with suffering, a crown awaits him. Though Christ was suspended on the cross, He was exalted. Though Timothy might be tempted to turn away, he must press on. Timothy is still in Ephesus, and he needs to complete his task. Paul reminds Timothy to continue the fight of faith, to be faithful to the end.

Second Timothy consists of three movements in which Paul encourages Timothy to persevere in the face of suffering. Paul urges Timothy to accept his calling and continue to be a good soldier for Christ (1:1–2:13). Then he explains that to do this, Timothy will need to challenge and correct the false teachers (2:14–4:5). Finally, Paul says farewell to Timothy (4:6–22). He promises Timothy that he will enter God's kingdom. A crown awaits him. Timothy needs to press on, looking to Paul's example and Christ's sacrifice.

2 TIMOTHY / FAITHFUL TO THE END

ACCEPT CALLING   1–2

Paul urges Timothy to press on in the ministry despite hardship.

Timothy's Calling   1:1–7

God appointed Timothy and gave him a spirit of power.

Not Ashamed   1:8–18

He should not be ashamed of suffering for the gospel.

Good Soldier   2:1–13

Persevere as a good soldier, athlete, and farmer.

CONFRONTATION   2–4

Timothy needs to challenge and correct the false teaching.

Correct   2:14–26

He must not quarrel but correct his opponents.

False Teachers   3:1–9

They appear godly, but they deny God's power.

Preach   3:10–4:5

Timothy is to preach the Word and embody true love.

PAUL'S FAREWELL   4

Paul's departure is near, but a crown awaits him.

Departure   4:6–8

Paul's life is "being poured out as a drink offering."

Circumstances   4:9–18

Though in prison, Paul will be safely brought to God's kingdom.

Closing   4:19–22

He finishes with a blessing; he has completed his race.

ACCEPT CALLING (1–2)

Paul begins by urging Timothy to accept his calling, especially in relation to suffering for the gospel. Timothy, like other Christians, is called to endure for the sake of Christ. To have the fortitude for this, Timothy needs to recall his history (1:1–7). The faith was passed down from his family, and he was given a spirit of power. He should not be ashamed of suffering, for God's calling and His people's suffering go hand in hand (1:8–18). Finally, Paul tells him to endure by being a good soldier, athlete, and farmer in God's economy (2:1–13). Essentially, Paul commands Timothy to press on. This is his calling. This is his destiny.

Timothy's Calling (1:1–7) / Though suffering awaits, Paul starts by encouraging Timothy to rekindle God's gift in his life. He gives thanks to God for Timothy's calling. Timothy is Paul's ministry partner, and he longs to see him. He emboldens Timothy to press on by reminding him that he comes from a family of sincere faith. Paul is convinced that sincere faith resides in Timothy too. Paul prompts him therefore to rekindle the gift that God has given him through His installation. Timothy has been given a spirit of power, love, and good judgment, not one of fear. He will need these virtues as he confronts false teaching and endures to the end.

Not Ashamed (1:8–18) / Timothy may have been tempted to be embarrassed by Paul and his suffering. Paul did not appear to be a man of power but one of weakness. Yet Paul reminds him that he has been called to share in the sufferings of Christ. The sufferings don't invalidate Paul's or Timothy's ministry; they authenticate it. Jesus Christ Himself appeared and suffered on behalf of His people, and now Paul imitates Him. This is also Timothy's calling. Paul is not ashamed of this vocation, and Timothy shouldn't be either. Paul trusts God will guard him to the end, and God will also do so for Timothy. Therefore, Timothy needs to be brave. He needs to hold tightly to what he has heard from Paul, recognizing that many have deserted Paul. The road ahead is tough, but God is faithful.

Good Soldier (2:1–13) / In the previous section, Paul instructed Timothy to not be ashamed of suffering. Now he turns to more positive instruction about being a faithful ambassador in God's army. Paul uses various metaphors to encourage Timothy's diligence. He is to be a good soldier, a competitive athlete, a faithful farmer. Despite hardship, all of these individuals are dedicated to their tasks. Likewise, Timothy is to be strong in the face of suffering and pass on Paul's teaching to later generations. Most importantly, he is to remember Jesus Christ and His suffering. If Timothy endures, he will reign with Jesus. If he dies with Him, he will live with Him. If he denies Jesus, Jesus will also deny him. But even if Timothy is not faithful, God will be faithful to him.

CONFRONTATION (2–4)

Paul transitions to commanding Timothy to confront and correct the false teachers (2:14–26). Some are veering from the truth and quarreling about words. But God's foundation still stands firm, even though some vessels in God's house are made for honorable use and others for dishonorable use. This indicates that the false teaching is coming from within the church, but these wolves are destined for destruction. Paul then describes the false teachers more extensively, giving a laundry list of traits and how they are sneaking their way into households (3:1–9). Finally, he contrasts the false teachers with Timothy's calling to suffer, preach the Word, and remain faithful to the gospel (3:10–4:5).

Correct (2:14–26) / Timothy has been given a commission. Paul contrasts Timothy's calling with these false teachers (2:14–19). Rather than fighting over words, Timothy is to correctly teach the word of truth. Rather than saying the resurrection has already come, Timothy is to remind them that God will rescue His people. God's firm foundation stands unyielding. Yet some in God's house are made for dishonor (2:20–21). Doctrinal and moral error comes from within God's church as well. Paul therefore exhorts Timothy to not be one of those made for dishonor, but to flee from their errors, to not be drawn toward sinful desires, to avoid foolish controversies. He is to put on kindness and gentleness. God may yet grant his opponents repentance (2:22–26).

False Teachers (3:1–9) / Though the false teachers have a chance to repent, Paul warns Timothy that the last days will be terrible. The opponents will be two-faced. They might look godly, but underneath the surface they deny its power. Paul gives a long list of the vices of the false teachers: lovers of money, selfish, proud, slanderous, not loving the good. Jesus said to love God and others; their love is misdirected. They sneak their way into homes and capture women who are burdened by sin. They tell women to neglect the things of the earth and claim these women sin by eating certain foods or marrying. They entrap people in their lies. They are like the Egyptian magicians, Jannes and Jambres, who opposed Moses. While it might look like they are doing similar things to Timothy, time will reveal the truth. God's rescuing power will be revealed.

Preach (3:10–4:5) / The false teachers have misdirected love, but Paul provides a different path for Timothy. He is to teach and embody true love. Paul is a model of this. Rather than serving himself, Paul's life is sacrifice through and through. Timothy is to follow Paul's teaching, way of life, faith, patience, love, endurance, persecutions, and sufferings. Suffering is central to God's calling. It is how Timothy loves God's people. Timothy is to continue in what he has learned from the Scriptures (3:10–17). Paul closes with a charge: Timothy is to preach the Word (4:1–5). Timothy should not only follow Paul's life, but his teaching. The time will come when people won't want to hear the message. But Timothy is to press on and "do the work of an evangelist" (4:5).

PAUL'S FAREWELL (4)

Paul closes his final letter speaking of his departure. His life has been full of suffering, but he has been faithful to the end. There have been opponents to Paul's ministry as well, but he has fought the fight and finished his race. Now a crown awaits him. Crowns also await all who persevere through suffering. The righteous judge sees all and will reward all those who have faithfully waited for Jesus, remained true to Him, and stood fast.

Departure (4:6–8) / Paul compares his expiring life to a sacrificial offering. He is being poured out as a pleasing aroma to the Lord. The time of his death is near. Yet though things look grim, Paul knows he has finished his race well. A reward lies in store for him. A crown of righteousness. While the false teachers spread lies and unrighteousness, the true Judge will reward Paul on the last day. Though the end is near, hope resides.

Circumstances (4:9–18) / In typical fashion, Paul closes the letter with notes about travel and greetings. Yet key themes of the letter also arise. Paul has endured suffering, but not all of Paul's companions have been faithful to the end. Demas abandoned Paul because of his love for the world. Alexander has also done harm to him. Everyone abandoned Paul when he needed them. People will likely abandon Timothy as well. But the Lord was with Paul and will bring him safely into the kingdom. Paul's simplicity of life and suffering is also evidenced by his requests. He wants his cloak, scrolls, and parchments while in prison. He still desires to encourage the church as he nears death.

Closing (4:19–22) / In his final words, Paul tells Timothy to greet his coworkers and asks for Timothy to come to him. These are the last words we have from Paul. He has fought the fight and finished the race. Because of his suffering, a crown awaits him in heaven. Timothy is to follow Paul's example. He is to be faithful to the end.

TITUS

BELIEF & BEHAVIOR

Consistency in confession and
conduct is paramount.

Behavior must follow belief, or belief is useless. Doctrine must support duty, or duty is empty. To divorce the two is an act of violence. Jesus died not so His people could live any way they wanted, but to cleanse them, make them zealous for good works, and create a community distinct from the world. Jesus rose to make a new people, a new society, a new future.

False teaching and the Cretan story concerning the Greek gods was soaking into the beliefs and behavior of the church in Crete. Paul sends Titus to appoint new leaders who live unlike the Cretan culture and confront false teachers (1).* He then urges the Christians to live blamelessly in the church and the world. He founds these instructions on the salvation brought by Christ, who purifies them, and the Holy Spirit, who washes them (2–3). Ultimately, he argues the Christian story is the only consistent foundation for devotion to good works.

_____

* "Titus," BibleProject, https://bibleproject.com/learn/titus/.

TITUS / BELIEF & BEHAVIOR

Faithful God   1:1–4

Paul contrasts the faithfulness of God to Zeus.

TITUS'S TASK   **1**

Paul instructs Titus to set things in order in Crete.

CHURCH CONDUCT   **2**

They are to exemplify gospel virtues in the church of God.

WORLD CONDUCT   **3**

They are to exemplify gospel virtues in the world.

Appoint Elders   1:5–9

Titus needs to choose qualified leaders in conduct and confession.

Proper Living   2:1–10

Titus is to teach respective groups "what accords with sound doctrine."

Ideal Citizens   3:1–3, 9–11

They are to submit to the government and be eager to do good.

Confront Liars   1:10–16

Silence the deceivers and liars who upset households.

Gospel Basis   2:11–15

Jesus appeared to make His people eager for good works.

Gospel Basis   3:4–8

The Holy Spirit came to wash and renew them.

Good Works   3:12–15

They need to devote themselves to good works.

Faithful God (1:1–4) / Paul begins by contrasting the faithfulness of God with that of Zeus to spur on good works. Though Zeus is never mentioned explicitly in the letter, Cretans held that the majority of gods were born on their island, including Zeus. They believed Greek gods were men and women elevated to deities. Zeus was a liar and a womanizer. Paul's writing to Titus is put against the background of Crete's sub-Christian value system. Paul argues knowledge of the truth in Christ leads to godliness. God, unlike Zeus, never lies and gives hope of eternal life, and now this message has been manifested in Paul's preaching. The faithful God compels faithful living.

TITUS'S TASK (1)

To further support these good works, Paul assigns Titus the task of appointing new leaders who live in contrast to the Cretan culture around them. The elders are to confront corrupt leaders who have been taken by the Cretan story. He commands Titus to put things in order and appoint elders, listing the qualifications for their position (1:5–9). These are put into contrast to the behavior of the false teachers (1:10–16). The emphasis is on the leaders' conduct and confession. They must be above reproach but also hold firm to sound doctrine so they can rebuke false teachers and embody faithfulness.

Appoint Elders (1:5–9) / Titus was left in Crete to put a chaotic situation in order. This included appointing leaders in every town. But these can't just be any leaders. He needs to appoint elders who have not been taken in by the false teaching or deceptive works. They need to have consistency in their confession and conduct. Many of the qualifications concern their character: faithfulness in their homes and in society. Twice he says they need to be above reproach. But he also affirms they must hold fast to sound doctrine and be able to rebuke those who contradict the message of Jesus. The leaders should be able to contend for the faith without being contentious.

Confront Liars (1:10–16) / The foil to the appointed elders is the false teachers. Some in Crete need to be silenced, as they are capturing whole families with lies. There are certain Jews who deceive people with empty talk about Jewish myths. They seek prosperity. They had been Cretonized: characterized by lying and cheating. Titus needs to shut them up and rebuke them so the congregation can have their belief and behavior cohere. Titus can identify the false teachers not by looking at what they profess but by examining their works. Their deeds will reveal their hearts. Professed faith that does not lead to godliness is dead and dangerous.

CHURCH CONDUCT (2)

The typical Cretan household will not transform society. Rather, Paul tells Titus to have the members of the church demonstrate the saving power of the gospel by living out its virtues in daily life. A new society is emerging in the corrupt Crete, but they must continue to have their doctrine and duty align. Paul applies this to various groups in the church, telling them how they should live properly (2:1–10), and then says the purifying arrival of Jesus is the basis for this behavior (2:11–15). The church is a contrast society, a symbolic new assembly in the midst of Crete.

Proper Living (2:1–10) / Rather than spreading myths and lies, Titus is to teach what accords with healthy Christian instruction. He applies this teaching to older men and women, younger men, and slaves. Each group has a particular responsibility based on their station. Older men are to be reverent and healthy in the faith. Older women are also to be reverent, not slanderers, and teach what is good. Younger men are to be self-controlled and respectful. Slaves are to be submissive to their masters (Paul often wrote to people in bad situations, instructing them how to live in a fallen creation). Good conduct adorns the gospel of Jesus and allows them to be light set upon a hill. A new society is emerging in the midst of a dying one.

Gospel Basis (2:11–15) / Paul supports his argument for proper living by giving an overview of the gospel message. The gift of God has come, offering salvation to all people. This gift is a person: Jesus. Jesus' message commands certain conduct. Embedded in this message is the command to rid oneself of vices and to live self-controlled and godly lives while waiting for the return of Jesus Christ. It was Jesus who sacrificed Himself to make His people pure and zealous for good works. The gospel is not just a message for the past but a command for the present and hope for the future. Titus should be confident in this message. He should stand upon it with the authority of Christ.

WORLD CONDUCT (3)

Paul continues his instruction concerning proper living but turns to how those in Crete conduct themselves with outsiders. The church needs to be ideal citizens, obeying the government and doing good. This is contrasted to false teachers who spread chaos and division. Again, he bases this on the arrival of Jesus, who washed His people with the Holy Spirit. God can create followers who are His new temples, behaving appropriately as they sojourn through this world.

Ideal Citizens (3:1–3, 9–11) / Paul is not only concerned with the congregation's conduct in the church but also argues that their demeanor in the world needs to be above reproach. They are to adorn the gospel by being submissive to the government and ready for good works. This includes not gossiping or quarreling but showing respect to all people. These deeds didn't characterize them before the news of Christ came to them, but the power of the gospel has changed them. He contrasts their new behavior in 3:9–11 with those who quarrel, fight, and spread foolish talk. Those going down the wrong path need to be warned. If they don't listen, the church needs to separate from them so that their witness will be pure.

Gospel Basis (3:4–8) / Again, Paul bases his command for behavior on belief. Jesus came to purify His people by the washing of the Holy Spirit. Unlike Zeus, the Christian God is good and kind. He sent Jesus to save and cleanse. Zeus came down to sleep with women. Contrary to the Greek gods, Jesus didn't reward people for doing good but saved people by His mercy even when they were wicked. Not only that, but He washed them clean by the Holy Spirit, who has been poured out and is available to all. Titus can insist on good works because this is why Jesus came.

Good Works (3:12–15) / Paul closes the letter to Titus asking Titus and other coworkers to come to him once his other companions reach Crete. He reiterates his main command: "let our people learn to devote themselves to good works." The false teaching and influence of the Cretan culture was not to sidetrack Titus from the transforming effect of Jesus' arrival and the washing of the Holy Spirit. Titus was to inspire proper conduct and true belief.

PHILEMON

RECONCILIATION

Jesus' sacrifice makes enemies friends.

The letter to Philemon is insignificant in terms of world history. It concerns a ruptured relationship between a master and slave in a small town in Asia Minor—an event not uncommon in the ancient world. Yet it is incorporated into the Canon because through this story readers see how Paul embodies Christ's reconciling sacrifice. Paul does not develop his theology so much in this letter—he lives it. He becomes Christ, a mediator who will bear the wrongs and debts of Onesimus so that two parties can be reunited. Paul takes up Christ's cross. He wields his power and privilege for the sake of the marginalized.

Paul writes to Philemon after a split between the master (Philemon) and the slave (Onesimus). But now Onesimus has become a Christian through Paul's ministry. Paul therefore appeals to Philemon's Christian character and the new higher social order of the gospel. Paul could command Philemon what to do, but he would rather have Philemon act out of his own free will (8–14). At the same time, he puts pressure on Philemon and tells him to welcome Onesimus and refresh his heart in Christ (17–20). There might be a divine purpose to their separation (15–16). The brotherhood of Onesimus now trumps their worldly relationship. Hostility is put to death at the cross. Hospitality radiates from the empty tomb.

PHILEMON / RECONCILIATION

PRISONER 1–3

ENCOURAGEMENT 4–7

PAUL'S APPEAL   8–14

Paul reframes who Onesimus is to Philemon now that he is saved.

DIVINE PURPOSE   15–16

Philemon should realize the conflict may have a redemptive end.

PAUL'S REQUEST   17–20

Paul requests that Philemon welcome and refresh Onesimus.

Not a Command   8–9, 14

Paul could command Philemon, but he prefers to appeal to him.

Kinship   15–16

Philemon can have Onesimus back forever as a brother in Christ.

Charge It to Me   18–19

Paul will substitute himself for the wrongs of Onesimus like Christ.

The New Onesimus   10–13

Onesimus is now a brother, useful, and Paul's very own heart.

Refresh My Heart   20

Paul asks that Philemon refresh his own heart, Onesimus, by welcoming him.

GUEST ROOM 21–25

PRISONER (1–3)

Paul begins by noting he is a prisoner. In this he shows both his sacrifice for Christ and indicates his solidarity with Onesimus the slave. Not only that, but he affirms he is not primarily a prisoner of Caesar, but a prisoner of Jesus Christ. He subtly informs Philemon that the Christ-event reshapes the social and political order. Paul continues with this recontextualization of the social order by describing his new family: Timothy is their brother, Apphia their sister, and Archippus their fellow soldier. Christ is creating a new social body that challenges the current structures of the day.

ENCOURAGEMENT (4–7)

Paul then thanks God for Philemon, foreshadowing many of the themes found later in the letter. Philemon is known for his love for all the saints and faith in Jesus (5). The hearts of the saints have been refreshed (or come to Sabbath rest) because of Him (7). Paul prays that Philemon's fellowship in the faith might become even more effective, alluding to his request at the end of the letter (6). Paul deposits honor into Philemon's account, and he will later "cash out" on more love, fellowship, and refreshment by asking him to show love, refreshment, and hospitality to his heart, Onesimus (17–20).

PAUL'S APPEAL (8–14)

Paul begins the body of the letter by lowering his position of privilege, thus exemplifying how he wants Philemon to act. He could command Philemon, but because he loves him, he would rather appeal to him for Onesimus (8–9). Then Paul describes the reversal wrought by the gospel in Onesimus. Onesimus is now a brother, child, and Paul's very own heart. The new situation calls for a new response (10–14).

Not a Command (8–9, 14) / Though Paul has the authority to command Philemon to welcome Onesimus, Paul decides it would be better for him to petition Philemon. He does this because he loves him and wants to see Philemon's faith become effective and grow through this difficult situation. Therefore, rather than employing his authority as an apostle, Paul seeks to lead Philemon to the good. Paul's leadership is one of empowerment rather than coercion (8–9). At the end of this section, Paul explains why he appeals to Philemon rather than command him. He wants the decision to be Philemon's, of his own free will (14). He desires Philemon's faith to grow as Christ compels him toward obedience.

The New Onesimus (10–13) / When Philemon hears the name of Onesimus, he likely first thinks of his status and the wrong he has done. However, Paul reframes Onesimus's status. His appeal is not for a slave, but for Paul's child and Philemon's brother. Familial language peppers the narrative, showing that Onesimus is now part of the family of God (10). God has given Onesimus a new birth. Not only is he a part of the new family, but he is a part of a new social order. Previously Onesimus was useless, but now he is useful (11). This is a play on Onesimus's name, which means "useful." Finally, Onesimus is Paul's own heart, his very being (13). In the thanksgiving section, Paul already praised Philemon for refreshing the hearts of the saints. Onesimus is part of a new family, a new society, and dear to Paul.

DIVINE PURPOSE (15–16)

Paul encourages Philemon to look at the state of things from a divine perspective rather than a worldly perspective. The conflict might have a greater end in view—in this case it looks like Philemon can have Onesimus back forever as a brother. The separation between them can result in a superior good. God is in the work of reconciliation. He turns what is evil into good. He makes all things new, even that which seems impossible. What looks one way at a worldly level looks different from heaven.

Kinship (15–16) / God is in the business of taking what is broken and marred, mending it, and making it even more beautiful. He uses the worst situations to accomplish the greatest good. In this case, Paul thinks the broken relationship may result in Philemon having Onesimus back not only as a slave but as a beloved brother (16). In the thanksgiving, he praised Philemon for his love; now Philemon can have a new brother both in the flesh and in the Lord. If Onesimus is now Paul's brother in the Lord, then he is also Philemon's brother. What Satan tries to destroy and distort, God will redeem. God's reconciling purposes can't be thwarted.

PAUL'S REQUEST (17–20)

Paul has not yet given his request, but finally he gets to the heart of the matter. Everything else has been set up. Everything else has been preparation. Paul requests three things in these verses, but his primary wish is the first one. He wants Philemon to welcome Onesimus (17). To do so, Philemon can charge the wrongs that Onesimus has done to Paul (18–19). This will refresh Paul's heart in Christ (20). It is by welcoming his heart

(Onesimus) that Paul's heart will be at rest. If there is any problem, Paul is willing to step into the gap and take the yoke upon his back because this is what Christ has done for him. Paul is a cruciform mediator.

Charge It to Me (18–19) / Paul's main request of Philemon is that he welcome and accept Onesimus (17). The hostility no longer needs to exist between them. But if this is to happen, the wrongs must be put right. The debt must be paid. Therefore, Paul affirms he is willing to take those wrongs on his own shoulders (18–19). If Onesimus has done anything wrong, Paul is willing to pay it. God is reconciling the world to Himself, and Paul is an ambassador not only spreading this message but exemplifying it. He takes up Christ's cross and forsakes his honor for the sake of the dishonored. Paul reaffirms who is writing this letter. His signature not only reminds Philemon of Paul's status but acts as an IOU that Philemon can charge the debts to. To put the pressure on Philemon, Paul also reminds him that he owes Paul his very life (19). Though Philemon might feel he is owed something from Onesimus, Paul flips the situation. Philemon is the client, and Paul is the patron. Ultimately God is the patron, and they are His clients. Philemon needs to act as God has acted toward him.

Refresh My Heart (20) / Paul affirms his love for Philemon and returns to some of the key themes he has already covered in the letter. He calls Philemon "brother," reminding him that he too is part of this new family. Then he calls him to "refresh [his] heart in Christ," the same word used for Sabbath rest. Already he has noted how Philemon has refreshed the hearts of the saints in the thanksgiving (7). Then he has called Onesimus his heart (12). Now he calls Philemon to again refresh the hearts of the saints (20). However, now the heart is both Paul and Onesimus, for Onesimus is Paul's heart. Philemon's fellowship in the faith will increase as he blesses Paul. To encourage Paul in this way is to act on behalf of his heart—Onesimus.

Guest Room (21–25) / Paul closes expressing the confidence he has in Philemon and also telling him that he is coming for a visit. Philemon must prepare a guest room for him (22). Paul will come soon to check and see how his appeal has been received. Then he sends greetings, including one from a fellow prisoner. Paul has not only taught of Christ, but became like Christ. The reconciling work of Christ expands in Paul's life. The hostility between a master and a slave is crucified in the Messiah.

HEBREWS

SUPERIORITY
OF THE SON

The temptation is to turn back to what is known, what is easy, what is traditional.

Hebrews warns readers to not fall away from the superiority of Jesus Christ. Though the author of Hebrews is unknown, the subject is not. Hebrews is a sermon explaining how Jesus is superior to the old covenant system and a call to not fall away. The focus is on the law and priesthood, giving the most detailed argument in the Bible for Jesus as the Great High Priest, who has gone into heaven and now intercedes for believers. All can draw near to God through Him.

Hebrews contends that Jesus is superior to various Old Testament systems, and therefore warns readers to not fall away from Christ. The first four verses give the point in short: Jesus is the superior revelation (1:1–4). The rest of the sermon explains how. Jesus is superior to the angels who mediated the law (1–2); therefore they need to pay closer attention. Jesus is superior to Moses (3–4); therefore they need to watch out that they don't harden their hearts. Jesus is the superior priest unstained from sin and serving in a better tent (5–7); therefore they need to mature. Jesus is the superior sacrifice and covenant who purified His people once and for all (8–10); therefore they should draw near to God. The author closes by telling them to persevere, looking to Jesus as their forerunner (11–13).

HEBREWS / SUPERIORITY OF THE SON

SUPERIOR WORD 1:1-4

Christ, the superior revelation.

Angels 1-2
....
Superior to angels.

Moses 3-4
....
Superior to Moses.

Priest 5-7
....
Superior High Priest.

Sacrifice 8-10
....
Superior sacrifice.

Pay Attention 2:1-4
....
Be on your guard.

Watch Out 3:7-4:13
....
Don't harden your hearts.

Mature 5:11-6:12
....
Grow in the faith.

Draw Near 10:19-39
....
Enter through the curtain.

Hall of Faith 11
....
A cloud of witnesses.

Run the Race 12
....
Don't lose heart.

Final Appeal 13
....
Various commands.

SUPERIOR WORD (1:1–4)

Hebrews begins with comparison and contrast. Previously, God communicated to His people through the prophets; now He speaks through His Son. Jesus is the superior revelation. This is the foundation for the rest of the sermon. Jesus is better than what came before because of His more excellent nature and name. Jesus is the heir of all things, the Creator of all, the exact nature of God, and the upholder of the universe. He is more excellent because He is the greater prophet, priest, and king, but the focus is on His priestly nature. He has made purification for sins and sat down at the right hand of God. He has a received the name of Son, which is superior to all other names. The rest of the argument flows from the nature of the Son and His work.

Angels (1–2) / Jesus is superior to angels. Angels delivered the law; they were the mediators (Deut. 33:2; Acts 7:53; Gal. 3:19; Heb. 2:2). But now the Mediator of God's or Christ's law is the Son. His name is superior to theirs. Numerous quotes from the Old Testament support this. The angels worship the Son because His throne is forever and ever. None of the angels were ever told to sit at the right hand of God, but the Son is currently reigning in heaven. Angels serve, while the Son is supreme (1:5–14). He was made a man so that He could share in their nature and defeat death by enduring it. Now He helps mankind as their faithful and merciful high priest (2:5–18). Jesus was made lower than angels for a time, but now He reigns in heaven, crowned with glory and honor because of His suffering.

Pay Attention (2:1–4) / In the middle of the meditation on the Son's superiority to angels, the author warns his audience. He tells them to pay closer attention to what they have heard because if the law mediated by angels required punishment for transgressing it, then how much more will they be punished if they break the law of Christ (2:1–3). They have a new Mediator. God has confirmed and affirmed the reality of His Son by bearing witness with signs, wonders, miracles, and gifts of the Holy Spirit (2:4). They can trust this message, which was given through Jesus. If disobedience to the law was punished, then so will disobedience to the Son. In fact, the Son offers a better salvation, so the punishment will be worse if they turn away from God's unique Servant.

Moses (3–4) / Jesus is now compared and contrasted with Moses. Both angels and Moses were known as mediators of the law and associated with the temple. Moses was faithful as a servant, but Jesus is superior because He built the house, while Moses was simply a helper in God's house. Jesus is the cornerstone of His people, while Moses is a stone. Jesus is the Son, while Moses is the servant (3:1–6). As in the previous section on angels

(2:5–18), the author closes the section by returning to the high priest theme (4:14–16). Since believers have a high priest who has gone into heaven, they need to hold fast so that they don't fall like the wilderness generation. Their High Priest is able to sympathize with them, but He never sinned. They can therefore approach God's throne and receive help in time of need. The wilderness generation had no priest like the Son.

Watch Out (3:7–4:13) / In the midst of speaking of Moses's faithfulness, the author directly addresses Israel's unfaithfulness (3:7–19). The wilderness generation heard God's promises but fell in the desert. They did not enter God's rest because their hearts were hard. Therefore, the listeners should also be warned of an unbelieving heart. They might become like the generation that failed to enter God's Sabbath. The promise of rest still stands, so the people should fear that they not become like the rebellious generation (4:1–13). Israel's hard hearts kept them out of the promised land. But the promise of rest still stands for believers who follow Jesus. If Israel fell while following Moses, how much worse will it be for those who fall while following Jesus? Therefore, they should watch out. They too might perish.

Priest (5–7) / Jesus is not only superior to angels and Moses, but He is the superior high priest (6:13–20). Believers have a merciful and forever high priest. Jesus comes in the line of Melchizedek and learned obedience by suffering. In the old order, high priests were taken from among men, acted on behalf of men, and offered gifts and sacrifices (5:1–4). In the new order, Jesus was also appointed, but He did not have any weaknesses or sins, and He doesn't have to offer sacrifices for Himself (5:5–10). Though Jesus was appointed, He learned obedience as a man. He was made complete through His suffering. Jesus became an eternal priest after the order of Melchizedek (7). Melchizedek was a figurative eternal priest, and Jesus fulfills his role. Even Levites paid tribute to Melchizedek. The old priesthood is out of date and could not perfect. The new priesthood has arrived.

Mature (5:11–6:12) / The author wants to describe more about Jesus' superior priesthood, but he can't. His listeners are children in the faith. They need to mature. They should be adults, but they still need baby food. They should be teachers, but they still need elementary doctrine (5:11–14). Therefore, he urges them to grow up. They need to turn from old practices and go on to adulthood. For if they have been shown the truth and turn back again to the old ways, it is impossible to bring them back (6:4–8). If they don't bear fruit, they will be burned in the fire. Though the author warns them, he feels confident in their case. They have shown evidence of faith and love. He hopes they persevere, mature, and find life in the superior priest (6:9–12).

Sacrifice (8–10) / If the previous section proved that Jesus was a superior priest, then the next two chapters focus on the ministry of the priest. Jesus is the superior sacrifice who mediates a superior covenant. He ministers in the new tent. If priests are appointed to offer gifts and sacrifices, then Jesus offers His own body and blood. This shows that the first covenant had faults, for a second was needed (8:1–7). But the author explains that the fault was with Israel (8:8–13). In the first covenant only the high priest could enter the holy of holies. This shows the way to God was not open yet, and the sacrifices could only deal with the external (9:1–10). Jesus enters a better tent in heaven, He brings His own blood, which truly sanctifies, and He only has to enter once rather than repeatedly. Therefore, He is the Mediator of a new and better covenant (9:1–28). The Old Testament law was only a shadow; Christ is the substance. The blood of animals can't take away sins, but the body of Jesus can. A new covenant has arrived (10:1–18).

Draw Near (10:19–39) / Because Jesus is the better priest, with a better sacrifice, and the Mediator of a new covenant, the congregation should draw near to God with full assurance. They don't need the Old Testament rituals. They have a new and living way through the body of Jesus (10:19–22). They should therefore hold fast to the confession of the new covenant and consider how to encourage one another. The audience can only do this if they continue to meet together and remind one another of Christ's sacrifice on their behalf. If they turn back to the old system, judgment awaits. If people died under the Mosaic Law, how much more will people be punished under the new covenant (10:26–31)? Previously, they showed evidence of faith, so they shouldn't throw away their new life (10:32–35). They need to persevere (10:35–39).

Hall of Faith (11) / The audience has a heavenly cloud of witnesses encouraging them how to live on earth. Israel's history provides paradigms that serve as exhortations. The sermon is a call for perseverance and faith, a warning of what happens if one does not heed the admonitions. The hall of faith is a snapshot of enduring heroes of the faith. Though Israel had negative examples, they also have positive ones. First, the author looks at those who had faith in the unseen (11:1–7), then Abraham, the prime example, and his descendants (11:8–22), then to Moses and the exodus generation (11:23–31), and finally to a smattering of examples (11:32–40). The author encourages the readers to emulate these saints. The people of God in the Old Testament didn't have Christ, yet they had faith and endured persecution while waiting for the promises. The readers must imitate them. The Old Testament saints looked to what they could not see. The audience looks to what has come.

Run the Race (12) / The final and climactic example of endurance in the race is Jesus. Because the audience has this cloud of witnesses, they should run the race set before them. They look back to the saints and to Jesus, who also suffered on the cross (12:1–3). The rest of the chapter expands on these exhortations to endure. They should endure discipline for holiness. This suffering is the discipline of the Lord to strengthen their faith (12:4–11). Therefore, they need to run, to fortify their hands and knees, to not falter in the race. This means being at peace, having holiness (12:12–17). If in the Old Testament Israel came before God at Mount Sinai and feared, they now come before Mount Zion, which is a vast celebration with angels and the congregation of the firstborn (12:18–24). The final warning is to not refuse the one speaking to them. If the Old Testament saints didn't escape, how will those who reject Jesus (12:25–29)?

Final Appeal (13) / A collection of commands fills out the final chapter and functions as the epilogue. It expands on what was introduced in the previous chapter: the worship and fellowship of the church. The author begins with practical expressions of love in the church (13:1–6). Love expresses itself in hospitality, caring for those in prison and those suffering. Love also expresses itself in marriage. They should not abandon one another, because Jesus will never leave them. In the second section, he tells them to remember their leaders and the suffering of Jesus (13:7–19). They should remember and obey them. In terms of suffering, they should also remember Jesus. Jesus also suffered outside the camp, so they should go out and endure with Him, for this is not their final home. The author's final words call them to prayer, point to Jesus as their Shepherd, and give a final exhortation, greeting, and benediction. Jesus will strengthen them (13:20–25). He is their high priest gone into heaven before them. They can approach God with confidence.

JAMES

WISDOM FOR WHOLENESS

Faith puts on flesh.

Wholeness does not occur until faith and action are integrated, until the outer and inner life match. There is no such thing as true faith that is not embodied in everyday life. James is a wisdom teacher who dispenses knowledge on a variety of topics as he applies the gospel to various circumstances, but it all sits under the theme of trials of faith. Though the half brother of Jesus didn't come to faith until after Jesus' ministry, he bestows lessons in line with Jesus' teaching and the Old Testament wisdom tradition.

James offers wisdom from above so that his readers might have lives that are whole. The structure of James is more haphazard, topical, and difficult to discern than many of the New Testament books. However, there is cohesion in that chapter 1 introduces the main theme, testing for wholeness, and covers in brief many of the topics that will be expanded later in the letter: anger, the tongue, the rich and poor, wisdom, faith and works, and rewards. James introduces these themes, urging Christians to be not only those who hear but those who do.

JAMES / WISDOM FOR WHOLENESS

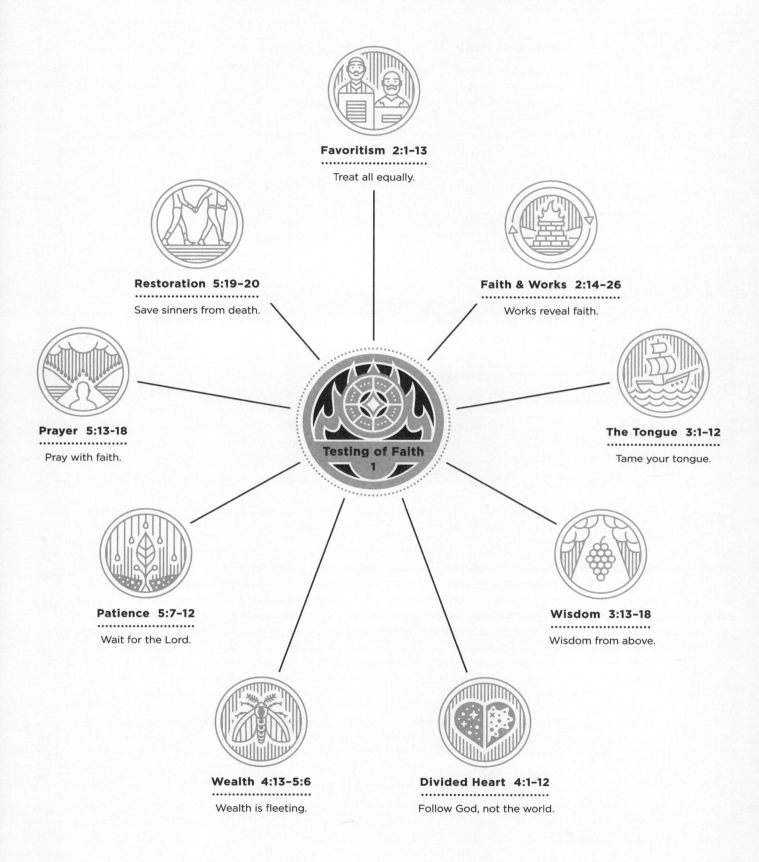

Favoritism 2:1–13
Treat all equally.

Faith & Works 2:14–26
Works reveal faith.

Restoration 5:19–20
Save sinners from death.

The Tongue 3:1–12
Tame your tongue.

Prayer 5:13-18
Pray with faith.

Testing of Faith 1

Wisdom 3:13–18
Wisdom from above.

Patience 5:7–12
Wait for the Lord.

Wealth 4:13–5:6
Wealth is fleeting.

Divided Heart 4:1–12
Follow God, not the world.

Testing of Faith (1)

James begins with the theme of the testing of faith. He argues it will unexpectedly produce wholeness in life. Therefore, they should count it a joy when trials come. Though many view the different sections of James 1 as disconnected, it is a coherent treatment of the theme of temptation. It also introduces, in brief summary, most of the themes that will be expanded on in the rest of the letter. In 1:2–12 he asserts the importance of fortitude in temptation since it produces completeness. They need to call out to God in these hard times, knowing that God will grant wisdom. The rich shouldn't rely on their riches but trust in God. Conversely, 1:13–18 issues a warning about distorted human desire, which can lure people away from relying on God's providence in their lives, especially during these hard times. They should not think God is tempting them during trials, because God only gives good gifts. Finally, 1:19–27 introduces three practical implications of trusting God in trials: quick to listen, slow to speak, and slow to anger. The temptation is to be quick-tempered during these times, to speak out of turn, but James tells them to trust God. These trials come into their lives to make them whole.

Favoritism (2:1–13) / Favoritism is a temptation in every age. Humans are prone to lift up some groups and reject others. James tells his readers that the way of Jesus is to not show partiality. In this context, it relates specifically to the poor. James returns to the topic he already introduced in 1:9–11, indicating his readers are poor and oppressed by the wealthy (2:1–13; 5:1–6). James tells them not to show favoritism to the rich, because it goes against God's character (2:1–7) and violates the command to love one's neighbor (2:8–13). God shows no favoritism and even selects what is shameful to the world. Jesus also commanded them to love God and others (Mark 12:30–31; see Deut. 6:5). If they show partiality, they break the law of God. They sin. And now they are empowered by the Spirit to live out the law in freedom. They should show mercy, for if they show mercy they will also receive mercy. They need to act out their faith in the everyday.

Faith & Works (2:14–26) / James moves from the specific exhortation of showing favoritism to the broader principle of the relationship of faith and works (1:22–25). For James, theology supports and sustains practical implications. James argues faith without works is dead; they must come in tandem to be genuine. Though some claim to have faith, faith is revealed *by* a person's works. Works are the tangible expression of faith. They are the clothes on top of the flesh of faith. Mere intellectual assent to God is inadequate. Even the demons believe. What matters is the combination of faith and works. Abraham is a key example of faith and works coming together. Abraham believed *and* he was willing to sacrifice Isaac. Though it sounds as if James contradicts Paul when he says "a person is justified by works and not by faith alone" (2:24), they are addressing different situations. Paul speaks to those who want to add Jewish laws to faith, while James presses professing believers to act out their faith in keeping with their commitment to Christ.

The Tongue (3:1–12) / James now turns to dispensing wisdom on the use of the tongue. This was one of the topics under the banner of trials in chapter 1 (1:19–21, 26–27). The tongue is like a rudder on a ship: it is a small portion of the body but has an enormous impact. He begins by addressing teachers, who will be judged more strictly since they are leading people toward either truth or error. He then turns more broadly to the use of the tongue, arguing that the person who controls their tongue is complete or whole. Though the tongue is a small part of the body, it controls much. He gives three illustrations: a rudder on a ship, a bit in the mouth of a horse, and a spark that sets a forest afire. The tongue can be used for good and evil; many times it is employed for both. James exhorts them in this way to encourage them to be those whose inner and outer life are integrated and united. They can't be springs that produce both freshwater and saltwater.

Wisdom (3:13–18) / James again moves from the more specific instruction (tongue) to the more general principle (wisdom). He extols the virtues of wisdom, a topic he brought up in 1:5–8 and 1:16–18. God gives wisdom to those who ask. Wisdom is shown in its results. The tongue can set a whole forest ablaze and be used to curse others, but wisdom that comes from above produces fruit. This fruit is embodied in gentleness, peace, purity, and openness. That which comes from the devil is full of strife, jealousy, disorder, and selfishness. Interlaced in this section is one of James's main themes: faith will reveal itself in works. He simply puts this point in a different chord, saying that there are two types of wisdom. Wisdom that comes from God or from Satan. The wisdom from Satan will manifest itself in fighting; the wisdom from God will manifest itself in peace. The overriding quality of wisdom is peace. True faith will be bathed with peaceful relationships.

Divided Heart (4:1–12) / The trials facing James's readers were not only external but internal. Fights and quarrels revealed their divided hearts. This continues the two themes alluded to in previous sections: the use of the tongue and wisdom full of peace. Now James directly addresses the disputes within the congregation. Some were jealous and coveting other people's things, maybe alluding back to the rich and poor in the congregation. James tells them that they can't have the values of the world and also be friends of God. They need to be complete Christians. They need to have their inner and outer life match. They need to submit themselves to God, resist the devil, draw near to God, and cleanse themselves from sin. Double-mindedness destroys people. People can't follow the world and follow God at the same time. Repentance and humility are the only way forward.

Wealth (4:13–5:6) / Now James turns and directly addresses the wealthy, saying their wealth will not last but will be moth-eaten (5:2; see also 1:9–11). He warns them to not depend on their wealth (4:13–17). They need to live in dependence on God and not be arrogant because of their success. The wealthy make their plans and suppose they will get rich, but all things come from the hand of God. James castigates the wealthy like a prophet. Some even think he has been addressing the rich Christians in 4:13–17 and now he turns to the non-Christians, the ones persecuting James's readers in 5:1–6. He tells them to lament what is about to come upon them (5:1–6). Misery and judgment lie ahead. Their riches will not stand on the last day. The moth has a way of making everything rot (Matt. 6:19–20). Gold corrodes. Houses fall into disrepair. Though they have laid up wages for themselves, their wealth will be given to another. They have cheated their workers, and justice will be demanded of them on the last day from the Lord of armies. God hears the cry of the righteous poor, and He will punish those who oppress the poor.

Patience (5:7–12) / Like some of the previous sections, James concludes with an exhortation toward patience and endurance in a sinful world. Though the rich oppress the congregation, they need to be patient and wait for Jesus' return. Not everything is as it seems. Jesus will make things right in the end. They need to be like a farmer who waits for his crops to arise. While the farmer waits, he waters and fortifies his field so that no destroying element will ruin his crop. In the same way, they need to live ready and prepared: without grumbling and remembering the prophets who waited for the coming of Jesus. They remained steadfast under trials. Look at Job. He waited, and God was merciful and gracious to him. They therefore need to be people of their word, who wait on the coming of the Lord with hearts steadfast in trial.

Prayer (5:13–18) / James closes by hitting a variety of topics: suffering, joy, sickness. Each situation has its appropriate response. This section focuses especially on prayer. If someone is suffering, they need to pray. If they are sick, the elders need to come and pray for them and pour oil on them. Many wonder at the significance of anointing oil, but most think the oil was a symbolic representation of someone being marked out for specific prayer. If they doubt the power of prayer, they need to remember the story of Elijah, who prayed that it might not rain, and it did not rain for over three years. Then he prayed again, and rain fell from heaven. Elijah was a human being, but he prayed in faith. So too, James's readers need to pray, trusting God's faithfulness.

Restoration (5:19–20) / The final topic James addresses is restoring those who wander from the faith. Though this might seem disconnected, the theme of action continues. In a successful intervention, a soul is saved and many sins are averted. Spiritual benefits result from a restored brother or sister. James's readers should not only follow what he has commanded, but make sure others do so as well. In this way, trials won't produce death for the congregation, but life, wisdom, and wholeness.

1 PETER

HOPE AS EXILES

Marginalized yet chosen.
Shamed yet honored. Insulted yet blessed.

Paradoxes fill 1 Peter. It is a letter written to encourage a slandered and marginalized minority living in the midst of the Roman Empire. They live in the world but are not of the world. They dwell in the cities, but as sojourners. They look, speak, and dress like everyone, but they pass their days on earth as exiles waiting for their inheritance" (see *Epistle to Diognetus* 5).

Peter seeks to encourage believers in Asia Minor in the midst of suffering to stand firm as they consider the blessings of being in Christ, who is the primary example of one who suffered well and now has received glory and honor. If they also continue in their good conduct, become the true household of God, and don't revert to their old idolatrous practices, they too will receive the crown of life. They need to have hope as exiles (1:3–2:10), live faithfully as exiles in the world (2:11–4:11), and stand firm until the end (4:12–5:11). Their ultimate enemy, that roaring lion, stands ready to devour them, but they have the conquering, suffering Shepherd at their side.

1 PETER / HOPE AS EXILES

ELECT EXILES 1:1–2

HOPE AS EXILES 1–2

The church has hope amidst trials because of their new future and family.

STAND FIRM 4–5

To keep their exile identity, they must stand firm to the end.

EXILE IDENTITY 2–4

In the midst of the world, they are to live as chosen exiles.

New Future 1:3–12

Their new birth grants them an inheritance that can never be taken away.

Submit 2:11–3:7

They are to submit to authority figures because this is how Christ acted.

Suffer Joyfully 4:12–19

They are to entrust themselves to God while doing good.

New Family 1:13–2:10

Their new birth grants them the rights and responsibilities of God's people.

Suffer Well 3:8–4:11

Like Christ, they are to suffer for good because suffering leads to life.

Resist the Devil 5:1–11

The elders should shepherd the people, recognizing the danger they are in.

IN BABYLON 5:12–14

149

ELECT EXILES (1:1–2)

Peter presents the paradox in the first two verses. To God, those in Asia Minor are chosen, but to the world, they are exiles and sojourners. This becomes the theme of the letter (1:17; 2:11; 5:13). It also ties their story to Abraham, who was chosen but also a sojourner on the earth (Gen. 15:13), and Israel, who were God's wandering people. These elect exiles are dispersed across Asia Minor and living in societies not friendly to the new Christian faith. They are elect exiles according to God's foreknowledge, by His sanctifying work, and chosen for obedience. This is God's wonderful plan for their lives.

HOPE AS EXILES (1–2)

After labeling them as elect exiles, Peter's first section bolsters their hope by praising God for their new future, new family, and new calling. Those scattered have been born again and promised a new land. But this new hope cannot be taken away from them because it resides in heaven. Though they suffer now, they are being guarded for this future (1:3–12). Not only do they have a new future but a new family and calling (1:13–2:10). They are the new exodus people, the new covenant people, and the new temple people. In all of these they have not only a new identity but a new vocation.

New Future (1:3–12) / Though their status as exiles is a dark backdrop, this reality is drowned out by their new hope as God's people. Peter therefore encourages them by praising God for their impending inheritance. First, he shows them that salvation brings hope (1:3–5). Their new birth has given them a living hope, an inheritance, a future salvation that can never be taken away. Even though they suffer, their future home is secure. Their salvation also brings joy even in the midst of trials because suffering purifies them (1:6–9). They are like gold being refined in the fire. Finally, their salvation brings hope because they stand at a privileged place in salvation history: the other side of the cross and resurrection (1:10–12). They now see what the prophets longed to see, and therefore they should praise God—despite their suffering in the present time—because their future is secure and brighter than they could imagine. Though this is a suffering community, Peter begins with praise because they have been welcomed as the people of God.

New Family & Calling (1:13–2:10) / If the first section was about how those in Asia Minor have a new future and therefore can praise God even in the midst of trials, this section further clarifies their new identity but also calls them to be holy. Their new family identity summons them to a new way of life. By using categories from the Jewish Scriptures, Peter forms their imagination and includes Gentiles in the story of God's people. They are the new exodus people who are called to have hope and be holy (1:13–21). They are the new covenant people who have gone through the waters and are to love and long for God (1:22–2:3). They are the new temple people who are being built up (2:4–8). And finally, they are the kingdom people who are to be holy and worship (2:9–10). The foundation of both their identity and ethics is Christ. Their new exodus identity is based on the blood of the Lamb, their new covenant identity on the enduring Word of God, and their new temple identity on the rejected stone. Peter skillfully shows the paradox of Christ is the paradox of their lives. Blood leads to life, the Word endures in exile, and the cornerstone is rejected but glorified.

EXILE IDENTITY IN THE WORLD (2–4)

After encouraging Gentiles concerning their new hope, Peter turns to how to live as exiles in the midst of a pagan society. Essentially, he calls them to resist sinful practices and to have honorable, virtuous, and good conduct. They are to do this in various spheres of life, and these good works are largely identified as submission rather than retaliation, perseverance rather than vacillation. Keeping their exile identity on this earth means looking to Christ's example of suffering and doing good even to those who mistreat them.

Submit (2:11–3:7) / Living as exiles means various temptations will face them. Therefore, Peter calls the believers to good works in their respective spheres and puts this under the banner of submission. Citizens are to submit to the government (2:13–17), slaves to masters (2:18–25), wives to husbands (3:1–6), and husbands are to respect their wives (3:7). They are to submit to governing authorities because in so doing they submit to the Lord. Yet all these actions are also subversive. They are to honor the emperor, yet also honor everyone. Wives are to submit to husbands, yet the goal is that their husbands will forsake their pagan practices and turn to Yahweh. Central to this section is the example of Christ as the "faithful slave and citizen" who subjugated Himself to unjust authorities (see 2:21–25). Not only is He an example, but His sacrificial body was their substitute.

Suffer Well (3:8–4:11) / Peter turns to more general comments under the banner of suffering well. They are to live righteously, not paying back evil for evil, but blessing others so that they can inherit the kingdom. This type of behavior will lead to life (3:8–12). All these commands come in light of the slander that the community received for their new way of life. Because of their newfound faith, they would not fit into society as before and would be called haters of mankind (see Tacitus, *Annals* 15.44). They are thus to suffer for righteousness' sake (3:13–17), not for evil (4:1–6), and live in light of the nearness of the end (4:7–11). They are to be sober, love one another, show hospitality, and serve one another. As in the previous sections, Peter uses Christ as the primary example for all these ethical admonitions. Christ is the true David, who kept His tongue from evil and saw good days (3:10–12). Christ is also the true Enoch, who ascended into heaven (3:18–22). He proclaimed victory over the spiritual forces of darkness and now has been glorified. He suffered in the flesh, but God exalted Him, and those in Asia Minor must also go through the ritual of baptism symbolizing the move from death to life.

STAND FIRM AS EXILES (4–5)

Peter closes his letter to this new community speaking about how they can keep their exile identity in the midst of fiery trials. They are to suffer with joy, knowing that suffering is God's way of refining them. Leaders in the congregation are to care for the flock as shepherds, following the example of Christ. All of them are to be humble and alert, taking their stand against their true enemy, the devil. Their inheritance awaits them. They simply need to stand firm.

Suffer Joyfully (4:12–19) / Peter begins the final section with another reflection on suffering. He tells them that the purpose of suffering is to refine them, as he did in the opening of the letter. Their hardship is a purifying and proving fire. Their response should be joy because in the midst of suffering they are blessed. Peter reiterates what he has stated earlier: they should suffer not for evil but for being a Christian. Suffering is a part of God's judgment and acts as a purifying force for God's people. If they are saved through flames, then what will happen to their accusers? Implied in his words are that the flames will destroy rather than refine those who are opposed to Christ. The flames have a dual purpose: destruction or purification. Therefore, those in Asia Minor should entrust themselves to their faithful God in the midst of hardships and look to their reward.

Resist the Devil (5:1–11) / Peter closes the letter by addressing first the leaders and then the entire congregation. Elders need to help their flock through this trying time. They are to shepherd them with pure motives and be a good example to those in their care. They also must remember they are simply undershepherds: Christ is the true Shepherd who will lead this people out of the valley of the shadow of death (5:1–5). All of the congregation is to be humble and alert, taking their stand against the devil. Though the Gentiles are the ones persecuting them, Peter reminds them of the dark supernatural force behind their suffering. The devil is a lion and seeks to consume them. However, at the same time, this suffering ultimately comes from the hand of God, so they are to cast their anxieties upon Him (5:6–11).

ENDURE IN BABYLON (5:12–14)

In the end, Peter reminds them that they are not the only ones living in exile. All Christians share the same identity. The church in Rome (Babylon) greets them (5:12–14). Peter's call for this marginalized, slandered, and suffering community is to stand firm because of the hope they have in Christ, even while they live in the midst of false cities waiting for their true home. The peace of Christ will be with them.

2 PETER

GROW IN GODLINESS

Jesus' fiery return compels godliness.

At the second coming, evil will be exposed and injustice destroyed as the new creation is established. Fire will dissolve the world and those who persist in doing evil will be judged. The life of Jesus and the prophetic testimony of the Old Testament both confirm this. Though people on earth wait, God will act in His own time, and there will be an end. Those who reject Jesus will be removed. Those who persist in good works will inherit the kingdom.

Peter was near death and needed to address false teaching that was circulating in the church. Certain irrational teachers denied judgment and Jesus' return, and thus encouraged works of the flesh. Peter therefore urges the church to grow in the grace and knowledge of Jesus Christ. He awakens them by reminding them of his teaching concerning godliness and Jesus' return (1). Then he condemns the false teachers, affirming they will be judged (2). Finally, he confirms the second coming of the Lord but acknowledges it will be in the Lord's timing (3). The return of Jesus should prompt the pursuit of righteousness.

2 PETER / GROW IN GODLINESS

Power for Godliness   1:1–11

Peter tells them to confirm their election by pursuing virtues.

PETER'S REMINDER   1

Peter authoritatively confirms Christ will return.

FALSE TEACHERS   2

The false teachers are irrational animals enslaved by their passions.

DAY OF THE LORD   3

Peter awakens them to false teaching about Jesus' return.

Stay Awake   1:12–15

He awakens them by reminding them to be holy.

The Impact   2:1–3, 17–22

They secretly spread heresies about Jesus' return and judgment.

Denying the Day   3:1–7

The false teachers deny Jesus' return.

Jesus' Return   1:16–21

The morning star is confirmed by testimony and prophecy.

Judgment   2:4–16

God has shown He will judge the unrighteous.

The Lord's Timing   3:8–13

The day will reveal all actions in the Lord's timing.

God's Patience   3:14–18

God's patience allows them time to repent.

Power for Godliness (1:1–11) / This is Peter's farewell address to Christians scattered across Asia Minor. He tells those in Asia Minor to confirm their election by pursuing virtues that accord with godliness. God's power enables them to practice these qualities as they wait for Christ's return. Divine power resides in them. Therefore, they should continue to embody a life of good works: faith, goodness, knowledge, self-control, endurance, and love. These works give evidence of those who are in Christ. Peter will later contrast these actions with the deeds of the false teachers. By pursuing godliness, the church confirms their election and paves a path to enter the kingdom of Jesus.

PETER'S REMINDER (1)

As Jesus instructed him in the garden, Peter reminds them to stay awake and keep doing good (1:12–15). Though false teachers deny Jesus' return, Peter knows Jesus will come back. He gives two proofs for Jesus' return. First, his own testimony of seeing Jesus transfigured on the mountain confirms Jesus' glory, which will be manifest on the last day (1:16–18). Second, the prophecies from the Old Testament confirm Jesus' second coming. Prophecy is sourced not in man but in the Holy Spirit (1:19–21). Both of these should induce them to stay awake and keep on the narrow path.

Stay Awake (1:12–15) / Peter's pastoral farewell is full of passion. He reminds them of what he has always taught them. In one sense, Peter doesn't have anything new to say. But the temptation is to fall asleep. To drowse like he did in the garden with Jesus. So he wants to awaken them again (stir them up by way of reminder) to the quest for righteousness. As long as Peter is still on the earth, he will rouse them to this vocation. False teachers are creeping in, denying Jesus' return and the future judgment. Peter reminds them to stay awake because he knows he will soon be gone. They must be able to recall his words once he departs. Peter's words, Jesus' words, and the words of the Old Testament will keep them from destruction.

Jesus' Return (1:16–21) / The call to godliness is intimately connected to Jesus' second coming. Jesus' coming is like the rising of the morning star. Peter confirms Jesus' return by defending himself. He is not making this up. He knows Jesus will return because he saw His glory on the mountain when Jesus transfigured before them (1:16–18). Jesus' power and identity was revealed to him. He physically saw the reality of the glorious Son when the Father spoke from heaven, affirming that Jesus is Yahweh's Son. Peter heard God's voice from heaven, he witnessed it, he is not irrational. But they have an even more sure word than he did (1:18–21). The Old Testament prophecies have been confirmed in Jesus' life, death, resurrection, and ascension. Jesus has fulfilled all that was predicted about Him, and now they await His return. This prophetic word did not come from humans, but from God, who spoke through the Holy Spirit. They need to pay attention to these words because the morning star (Jesus) will rise in their hearts.

FALSE TEACHERS (2)

Peter turns his gaze to the false teachers and condemns them, calling them irrational animals who are enslaved by their own passions. But they will destroy themselves. The opponents spread heresy and deceive many. They promise life, but only offer death. They promise freedom, but exploit people. They seduce people, telling them to indulge in their filthy desires, but only offer slavery. But like the many examples in the Old Testament, they will be judged and destroyed when Jesus returns. They will not be spared on the last day. Therefore, the church needs to reject their teaching and press on toward holiness.

The Impact (2:1–3, 17–22) / The false teachers are like snakes who slither into congregations promising good fruit, but their fruit only leads to death and slavery. Like in the Old Testament, the community will be tested by adversaries. Many will follow their seductive speech as they seek to use the people for their own ends. Like the serpent in the garden, they promise springs of life. The result of partaking of their fruit is only thorns and thistles. They spread lies promising freedom, but people end up being slaves to their own passions. The false teachers are those who have learned of Jesus, but then corrupt this knowledge, making their last state worse than their first one.

Judgment (2:4–16) / Though the false teachers spread heresies, their destruction is sure. God's past actions prove this as Peter gives a catalogue of God's retribution from the Old Testament. He begins with the angels in Genesis 6 who sinned by coming to sleep with women on the earth. They were put into the underworld and kept in chains until the judgment (2:4). God not only judged the angels but the earth in the days of Noah. He overwhelmed them with the floodwaters while He provided a way out for Noah and his family (2:5). God also destroyed Sodom and Gomorrah with fire because of their immorality but saved Lot because of his righteousness (2:6–7). All of these examples involved sexual immorality, indicating that the false teachers may have been emboldening licentiousness in this realm. But Peter affirms that God rescues those who keep themselves pure. These false teachers reject authority and follow the path of Balaam. But God's people can't be cursed. They are promised blessings.

DAY OF THE LORD (3)

Peter finishes his farewell address by affirming that the day of Lord will come. It will come with fire that will reveal everyone's works. Though the false teachers encourage works of the flesh and deny Jesus' return, Peter reminds those in Asia Minor to stay awake in the face of these heresies. Though it might seem like God is not fulfilling His promise, they must remember God's timing is unlike theirs. One day is like a thousand years to Him. One day the Lord will return and rid the world of evil and injustice. Because of this, they should press on toward godliness and reject the desires of the flesh.

Denying the Day (3:1–7) / The false teachers deny Jesus' return. But Jesus will return and cleanse the earth by fire. Peter returns to language he used in 1:12–15. He wants to awaken them by reminding them of the message he already spoke to them through the prophets. Peter and the prophets both affirmed that false teachers will sneak into the church and deny both doctrine and devotion. Doctrinally, they reject Jesus' return. Devotionally, they follow their own desires. But Peter reminds them of creation and re-creation. The world was brought forth through water twice, once at creation and once in Noah's day. In the same way, the earth will be cleansed. In the last day, it will not be with water but with fire as those who deny Jesus are judged.

The Lord's Timing (3:8–13) / Peter affirms that the final day will reveal all actions in God's timing. Though they might wonder when the day of the Lord is, they must remember God's timetable is not theirs. One day is like a thousand years to Him. He has promised it will happen, and so it will. His patience allows people time to repent. But when He does come, it will be a surprise. On that day He will peel back the heavens and the earth and reveal all the works done on the earth. The heavens will be dissolved, and the earth will melt as He re-creates all things. It will be a day of disclosure. A day of judgment. A day of salvation. Because of this, the church needs to press on in confirming their election.

God's Patience (3:14–18) / Because the Lord's return is sure, those in Asia Minor need to be diligent concerning growth in godliness. While they wait, they should labor over their holiness and realize God's patience allows them to pursue Christian virtues. Paul has also written about these things, but sometimes Paul's writings can be "hard to understand" (3:16). Those who reject and twist the apostolic words to their own ends are headed for destruction. So the church needs to be on guard. They are not to be led astray by the soldiers of Satan who seek only their enslavement and death. Peter's last words are this: pursue growth in the grace and knowledge of Jesus.

1–3 JOHN

GOD IS
LIGHT & LOVE

Assurance is the stream
that flows from the spring of faith.

Or in the words of Stephen Charnock, "Assurance is the fruit that grows out of the root of faith." Believers need assurance. They need assurance that Jesus is who He claimed He was. That their sins are forgiven. That what they believe is true. John writes his three letters to comfort and soothe believers that they do possess salvation and have eternal life. To do this, he must go on the offensive against antichrists who don't believe Jesus is the Messiah and claim people are still in their sins. The opponents taught there is no connection between what one believes and how one lives. John affirms that God is light (truth) and love (action).

John doesn't write in a straight line in his three letters. His letters are circular. He introduces a theme and then returns to it. He weaves in other themes and then returns to them. John writes so that people might believe in the Son of God and so that they might have eternal life (1 John 5:13). To do this, he interlaces three basic themes of the Christian life: obedience, love, and truth. Because God is light (1:5), he wants his readers to walk in the light. Because God is love (4:8, 16), he wants his readers to walk in love. Their actions should be sourced in their belief about Jesus. John's letters are for the comfort and assurance of believers in light of those who had gone out from the congregation. Their hearts will confirm they are walking in the truth.

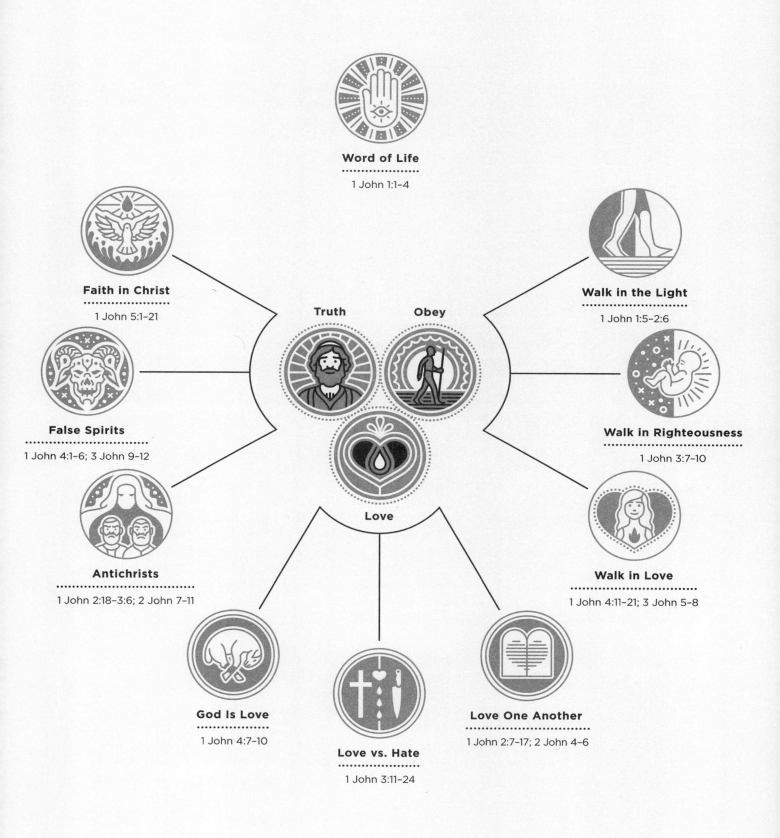

Word of Life

1 John 1:1–4

Faith in Christ

1 John 5:1–21

False Spirits

1 John 4:1–6; 3 John 9–12

Antichrists

1 John 2:18–3:6; 2 John 7–11

Truth

Obey

Love

Walk in the Light

1 John 1:5–2:6

Walk in Righteousness

1 John 3:7–10

Walk in Love

1 John 4:11–21; 3 John 5–8

God Is Love

1 John 4:7–10

Love vs. Hate

1 John 3:11–24

Love One Another

1 John 2:7–17; 2 John 4–6

Word of Life (1:1–4) / John begins by assuring them. He affirms that he has heard, seen, and touched Jesus. He calls Jesus the Word of life and links Him to the beginning, echoing John's gospel and Genesis. Jesus is the source of life. He is the Word who created life. He is eternal life. And now He has appeared on this earth in the flesh and John has seen and touched Him. John's readers can be assured they only have life in Jesus. They can be assured He is real. They can be strengthened in their faith because as they have fellowship with the apostles, so they have fellowship with the Father and the Son. What John writes to them is true.

Walk in the Light (1:5–2:6) / John turns to speak of God's nature and humanity's sin. God is light (1:5). He is true. Pure. Holy. Perfect. All practical theology must flow from confessional theology. John continues with his Genesis imagery. If God is light, they ought to walk in the light (1:5–10). If they walk in darkness, then they don't walk with Him. Yet if they say they don't have any darkness, they also lie. The false teachers must have been spreading instruction about the possibility of perfection. It is only through Jesus' blood that darkness is removed. John writes to them so that they might not sin, so that they might not walk in the darkness (2:1–6). But if they do, they must remember they have an atoning sacrifice for their sins. They should confess their sins and turn to Jesus since He is the Word of life, the Light of the World.

Love One Another (2:7–17; 2 John 4–6) / John said the love of God is made complete in those who walk in the light. Light and love are interwoven. Now he develops this even further, telling them that he writes to them not a new command but one they have had since the beginning (2:7–11). Yet it is also a new command because it has been manifested in Jesus. The command is to "love one another." Love and light are stitched together (2 John 4–6). So are hate and darkness. Light produces love. Darkness produces hate. John tells them to love each other because God is light. They must not love the world. They must love the Father. The false teachers may have been encouraging more cooperation with those outside the faith. John assures them of his purpose, speaking to various groups in the congregation (2:12–17). He writes to them because their sins are forgiven, because they know the Word of life, because they have overcome the darkness. They should be encouraged despite the presence of the antichrists.

Antichrists (2:18–3:6; 2 John 7–11) / Though John has indirectly addressed the false teaching, he now does so directly. He tells them the antichrist is coming, but there are also many antichrists who exist now. Antichrists are those who deny Jesus has come in the flesh (2 John 7–11). These people were a part of the community but have left. John's community must not be hospitable to them. But John's readers are different from them. They have the resources to abide in Christ. They have the Holy Spirit. They know the truth. They do not deny Jesus. It is those opposed to Christ who are headed toward destruction. The opponents are trying to lure the congregation away from Christ, but the "anointing" rests on the congregation (2:18–27). The congregation can be assured. Therefore, they must press on (2:28–3:1). They must be confident. They are clean because the Father has sent the Son to rescue His people and make them His children. And in fact, they are God's children.

Walk in Righteousness (3:7–10) / The implication of them abiding in the light, of being children of God, of having the anointing is that they can walk in righteousness. This is another way of speaking of walking in love and in the light. Actions and deeds reveal if people are in light or darkness. The one who does evil is of the antichrist. The one who commits sin is of the devil. But Jesus came into the world "to destroy the works of the devil" (3:8). Therefore, no child of God will continue in sin like these false teachers. The congregation can identify who is from God by their actions. They don't have to be confused or deceived. Love is the sign. People are either born of God or born of the devil.

Love vs. Hate (3:11–24) / Love is not primarily a feeling. It is displayed in words and actions. They can be assured they have the anointing by looking at the fruit of their lives. The opposite of love is hate. Cain murdered his brother because his deeds were evil and Abel's were righteous. Everyone who hates is a murderer. Everyone who loves is from God. Love is displayed on the cross. Their hearts will either confirm or deny the truth in them. If their hearts affirm their love for God, then they can have confidence because they keep God's commandments. They please Him in all things. The basics of Christianity are simple: believe in Jesus Christ and love one another. The one who does these things dwells in God, and God dwells in them by the Spirit.

False Spirits (4:1–6; 3 John 9–12) / John returns to the antichrists, speaking of them as false spirits and prophets. He says the opponents' teaching is sourced in deceitful spirits. He has already spoken about how those in the congregation have the anointing of the Holy Spirit, and now he contrasts that with spirits contrary to God. The way the church can identify the false spirits is by their confession. If these teachers affirm that Jesus came in the flesh and is from God, then they are from God. But if they don't, then these people are the antichrist. But the assembly can be assured because they are children of God. Those that deny Christ are from the world. But the one in them is greater than the one in the world. In 3 John he gives the negative example of Diotrephes, who will not welcome John, and the positive example of Demetrius, who knows the truth (3 John 9–12).

God Is Love (4:7–10) / Those who are of God love God. They also love one another because God is love. Those born of God know God. Those who don't love don't know God. God's love was defined and demonstrated in the sending of Jesus Christ. He loved by taking the first step. And He loved by dying upon the cross as an atoning sacrifice. He is the sacrifice for their sins, the definition of love. The triune God defines true love: the Father planned salvation, the Son accomplished it, and the Spirit applies it. God's actions in the economy of salvation are the foundation and spur for actions on the earth. Christians love because they have first been loved.

Walk in Love (4:11–21; 3 John 5–8) / Since God is love, since He loved the world by sending the Son and by the Son's sacrifice, Christians should love one another. This is how they know they abide in God and He abides in them. This is how they know if they have the Spirit of God. John returns to his own testimony here, saying he has seen and witnessed the coming of the Son into the world. If anyone acknowledges Jesus is the Son of God, then God lives in them. God is love. They love because God first loved. If someone claims to know and love God but hates a brother or sister, they lie. Believers can be assured of their right standing with God by their love. In 3 John, he praises Gaius's support for Christian workers even though they are strangers to him. Showing hospitality is showing love (3 John 5–8).

Faith in Christ (5) / John continues to speak about love, but he emphasizes faith as well. Faith is the foundation of love. This faith is centered on Jesus being born of God. Everyone who has faith, who is born of God, overcomes the world. Jesus came by water, blood, and the Spirit. He was baptized, died, and gave His Spirit. These three witness and testify to the God-begottenness of Jesus. God has testified through these three that Jesus is from God, and whoever accepts this testimony is from God and has eternal life. John writes that they might believe in the Son and have eternal life. John closes with a word about how to deal with sin in the congregation. There are sins that lead to death (denying that Jesus comes from God) and sins that don't. If they see someone sin in a way that does not lead to death, then they should pray for them and God will give them life. If they keep on sinning, they show themselves to be of the evil one. But John has confidence in his readers that they have true understanding. He testifies to the Word of life. He assures them they are in Christ.

JUDE

CONTEND FOR THE FAITH

Beliefs don't patrol themselves.
They must be fought for.

Though Jesus has come to earth, Christians still wait. Though the truth has been revealed, lies still circulate. Though Jesus has conquered, the end has not arrived. In the midst of waiting, different teachings of Jesus will arise. Many of these will not be according to the apostolic tradition. Jude, the half brother of Jesus, writes because the time has come to contend for the faith. Armor must be donned. The sword of the Spirit must be taken up. The shield of faith must be raised.

Jude wishes he could have written a different letter. But he must address false teaching. Dangerous opponents have disrupted the church, claiming Christians are free to do what they wish and also reject authority (5–16). Jude says the solution is to remember apostolic prophecy about the coming of such teachers and to keep themselves in the love of God by building a strong foundation, staying strong in prayer, and waiting for the return of Jesus (17–23). Jude's hearers are called, loved, and kept by God. God has secured their future. Therefore, they need keep themselves in God's love.

JUDE / CONTEND FOR THE FAITH

Called, Loved, Kept   1–2
....
Jude writes to those called, loved, and kept by God.

Contend   3–4
....
Jude must fight for the faith because of false teachers.

FALSE TEACHERS   5–16
_____

The false teachers are fruitless, directionless, and will be judged.

Judgment   5–7
....
Israel, angels, and Sodom were judged in the OT.

Nature   8–13
....
They are waves of the sea that destroy.

Judgment   14–16
....
Jesus will destroy them when He returns.

Prophecy   17–23
....
Jude says recall prophecy, and keep themselves in God's love.

Kept   24–25
....
God will guard them from stumbling till the last day.

Called, Loved, Kept (1–2) / Though Jude is Jesus' half brother, he begins by stating he is a slave of Jesus. Jude did not believe in Jesus until after Jesus' execution, but now he is a leader in the church. The specific location he writes to is unknown as he identifies his audience theologically. He writes to those who are called, loved, and kept. All of these characterizations emphasize God's action, His work in them. There is also a certain progression, a salvation order to his description. They have been called, they are loved, and they will be kept till the end. This theme of "keeping" arises two other times in Jude as he calls them to "keep" themselves (21) and how God is able to "keep [them] from stumbling" (24). The danger is that they might be swept away by the false teaching, but Jude is confident in God's work in them.

Contend (3–4) / Jude wished he could have penned a different letter. He wanted to encourage them, reflecting on the salvation that is theirs in Christ. However, a new situation has arisen. He must write and contend for the faith that was passed down from the apostolic circle. This word *contend* is an athletic and combat term. Jude must exert effort on behalf of those who believe. They are in danger, for certain teachers have snuck into the church who are destined for judgment. These teachers promote sexual excess and deny the Master Jesus. Jude is Jesus' servant, and he will do all he can to support and defend his Lord.

FALSE TEACHERS (5–16)

Most of Jude concerns his judgment on the intruders. Jude employs a variety of biblical images and analogies to describe them, including dead trees and wandering stars. Certain judgment is coming for these unreliable guides. The section begins and ends with judgment, and Jude's affinity for the number three is exemplified. He gives three historical examples of God's judgment (5–7), three sins warranting judgment (8–13), and finally closes with another word of judgment and a fuller description of the false teachers (14–16). These people are warped and perverted, but their end is sure.

Judgment (5–7) / Jude has already said that the false teachers encourage sexual immorality and deny Jesus. Now he gives three historical examples of God's judgment. First, the exodus story. Jude reminds them how God brought His people out of Egypt but destroyed that generation in the desert. His point is that no believing person can presume upon God's grace. They must persevere or they too will be destroyed. Second, Jude speaks of the fallen angels from Genesis 6. These angels had relations with with the daughters of men and were kept in Tartarus in chains of judgment. Even those in high authority are judged if they forsake the righteous path.

Third, he brings up Sodom and Gomorrah, which also indulged in sexual immorality and were judged. God's judgment upon those who forsake His ways is certain. God's track record is plain.

Nature (8–13) / The false teachers have only been described in brief. Now Jude fills out his descriptions with three sins warranting judgment. Throughout this section, Jude uses an abundance of allusions and metaphors to make his point. First, the false teachers defile the flesh through their sexual laxity and rely on subjective experiences rather than God's revelation (8). Second, they reject authority (8–10). He gives the example of the archangel Michael and the devil disputing over Moses's body. Michael didn't even pronounce upon the devil a sentence but said, "The Lord rebuke you!" Michael understood that God had the prerogative of judgment. Third, the false teachers are greedy (11). They are like Cain, Balaam, and Korah, who seek only their own blessing. Jude closes with a range of metaphors for the false teachers (12–13). They are hidden reefs, destroying ships that come too close. They are shepherds who neglect to feed their flock. They are waterless clouds that promise rain but never provide. They are fruitless trees. Wild waves of the sea that destroy. Wandering stars that lead people astray.

Judgment (14–16) / Jude declares woes upon the false teachers in a final condemnation and description. Enoch prophesied about teachers who would be destroyed by the Lord when He comes with His army. Jesus will come bearing the sword to all who deny His truth. Now Jude describes the false teachers with more descriptions, confirming their judgment. They grumble. They follow their own desires. They boast. They show favoritism. Sin is followed by more sin. Sin is a pollution that seeps into every corner, a disease that eats away at a person until their whole life is consumed and distorted.

Remember Prophecy (17–23) / Jude turns and addresses believers. He calls on them to do two things. First, they are to remember the apostles' prophecy about these teachers (17–18). The apostles said there would be ridiculers who cause divisions and who don't have the Holy Spirit. Their presence should not be a surprise. They should be ready for the intruders. Second, they need to keep themselves in the love of God (20–21). Already Jude has said they are kept (1), but here he says they have a part to play. Divine and human agency are not contradictory. Jude's hearers keep themselves in God by strengthening their faith, praying in the Holy Spirit, and waiting for the mercy of Jesus. However, Jude also reminds them how to treat others (22–23). They need to have mercy on those who doubt. A harsh and swift strategy is to be taken with the leaders, but grace is to be given to those who are confused. In fact, they are to pursue those affected by the teaching but make sure they are not ensnared by sin along the way.

Kept (24–25) / Jude closes with a doxology of comfort and hope. Though the false teachers have crept in. Though they teach what is opposed to God. Though they deny authority. God is able to guard Christians from stumbling. Christians are to guard themselves, but it is ultimately God who keeps them. Those whom God has called He will also glorify. God will present them as gloriously pure and blameless on the last day. Therefore, their whole life needs to be oriented toward praise to God the Father and the Son Jesus Christ.

REVELATION

TRIUMPH OF THE LAMB

Dragons. Beasts. A lion. A lamb. War.

The last book of the Canon is filled with mysterious imagery. However, the purpose is not to confuse but to reveal. Symbols illuminate rather than obscure. Revelation ends in a garden-city with the tree of life. God's temple presence is there. The river of life flows through the city. It is a new but better Eden, a new but better Jerusalem. However, to get to peacetime, war must ensue. The empires of the earth must fall and those who oppress God's people must be punished. The Lamb will triumph over the dragon and get His bride; God's people will be with Him forever. They must conquer and not be seduced by Babylon.

John writes to seven churches in Asia Minor, but these stand as symbols for all outposts of the kingdom. The first part of Revelation reads like an epistle (1–3) and then John enters God's throne room. Everything in the narrative emanates in circular fashion from the one on the throne and the Lamb (4–5). The seven seals (6–8), trumpets (8–11), and bowls (15–16) are God's progressive judgments on the nations, but in them God also shelters His people (7; 10:1–11:14). It is Satan who seeks to devour the church. The battle ends with the fall of the great city Babylon, which is opposed to God (17–20). Then comes restoration and renewal, the New Jerusalem and a new creation (21–22).

REVELATION / TRIUMPH OF THE LAMB

Epilogue 22:6–21

Prologue 1:1–8

New Creation 21:1–22:5

Seven Churches 1:9–3:22

Triumph 19:11–20:15

Throne Room 4–5

Seven Seals 6:1–8:5

Babylon Falls 17:1–19:10

Seven Bowls 15–16

Holy War 12–14

Seven Trumpets 8:6–11:19

Prologue (1:1–8) / Revelation begins and ends in a similar way: John explains that this apocalypse was revealed to him by an angel, but they are words from God Himself. Blessings are pronounced upon those who read and keep these words. Much of the book is a call to persevere and conquer. John greets the churches in Asia Minor from the triune God: the forever one (Father), the seven spirits (the Spirit), and the faithful witness (the Son). His focus lies on Jesus. The manifold description of Jesus proves this. Jesus is the faithful witness, the firstborn of the dead, the ruler, and the sacrifice. He is the prophet, priest, and king. The attention on Jesus continues, but now John gazes into the future. Jesus is coming back. Mourning will fill those who reject Him. Comfort will reverberate from those who welcome Him.

Seven Churches (1:9–3:22) / John then sees Jesus in the midst of lampstands (1:9–20). Jesus walks among His churches as the fulfillment of the Daniel 10 vision. John writes to these seven lampstands (the seven churches) as a messenger of the Son of Man (2–3). In each of them he gives a description of Christ, a commendation, rebuke, solution, consequences for disobedience, and promise for conquerors. For example, he describes Jesus as the one who holds seven stars, the First and the Last, the Holy One, and the originator of God's creation. He rebukes the church for forsaking their first love, tolerating false teachers, and not doing good works. But to the one who conquers He will give fruit from the tree of life, rescue from the second death, a new name, and white clothes. These churches are under attack and their spiritual vitality is in decline. They need to see the splendor of Jesus to conquer. If they do, they will receive rewards. If not, He will come with a sword.

Throne Room (4–5) / John is catapulted into heaven's throne room, where he sees the one on the throne (4) and the Lamb (5). It is an adoration ceremony. The rest of the book pulsates from this location. Around the one on the throne are worshipers: twenty-four elders, seven spirits, and four living creatures. These are cultic, creational, and political images. All these beings proclaim the sovereignty of the seated one. He is holy, the Creator, while they are creatures. The throne is described as full of luminous colors, flashes of lightning, and a sea of glass. It is an awe-filled, frightening, yet peaceful place. It is a place of worship. They worship the Creator of all. Chapter 5 transitions. Now John sees a scroll in the hand of the one on the throne. John now realizes it is a courtroom. The scroll represents redemptive history and God's purposes for creation. Blessings and curses will issue from the scroll. But the scroll can't be opened except by a worthy one. Only the Lion of the tribe of Judah, the Root of David, can open the scroll. John is told this one is a Lion, but he sees a Lamb. *This one* is worthy to open the scroll because He is covered in blood. He has been slain. The Lion/Lamb takes the scroll, and everyone worships. The seals, trumpets, and bowls will issue forth from this scroll, but so will the safeguards for God's people. Worship reverberates forth from the throne room, but this time to the Lamb.

Seven Seals (6:1–8:5) / The Lamb now opens the seven seals (6:1–8:5). These seven seals are judgments upon the earth and take place between Christ's resurrection and second coming. The white horse stands for victory, the red horse for war, the black horse for famine, and the pale horse for death. When seal five is opened, readers are again brought up to heaven, where the blood of the slain saints cry out for justice. How long till He destroys their enemies? God says wait a little longer. Seal six contains a final great earthquake and answers the call of seal five. This is the final wrath of the Lamb upon rebels. Creation crumbles. So who can stand in the face of this wrath? Those sealed by God will be kept from wrath. The interlude shows 144,000, or an uncountable multitude, will be preserved for the Lamb (7). These are God's people as a whole. The seventh seal is transitional. It shows the judgment of the trumpets is in answer to the cries of the saints. The seals, trumpets, and bowls all expand upon the same events.

Seven Trumpets (8:6–11:19) / In the Bible, the sound of a trumpet announced the coming of a war, a victory, or even a warrior. They could be warnings or victorious sounds. The trumpets in Revelation do all the above. They announce God's judgment upon the earth and its inhabitants, mirroring the plagues in Exodus. The first four trumpets speak of the sentence upon the earth (hail, fire, blood), sea (burning mountain in the sea), rivers and springs (burning stars on rivers and springs), and sky (sun, moon, and stars darkened). Cosmic destruction is underway (8:7–12). The strangeness of the scene only increases with trumpets five, six, and seven. Three woes are pronounced as demons come from the abyss (9:1–11). The locust imagery stems from Joel and portrays an army inflicting misery on unbelievers. But believers are sealed. The second woe (trumpet six) has demons from the east (9:13–21). This is humanity's last warning. The demonic horde slays and destroys. The judgments have escalated. As in the narrative of the seven seals, an interlude interrupts, where the people of God are depicted as prophetic witnesses (10:1–11). Their temple is protected (11:1–2), but the two witnesses will be persecuted. They will be saved from wrath, yet they will be conquered for a time (11:3–14). The final trumpet announces the end of history (11:15–19). The kingdom now belongs to God, Christ, and His people. Readers are back in the throne room worshiping with the twenty-four elders.

Holy War (12–14) / A complementary and transcendent perspective of the same events is offered. The war on earth is now described as a battle with Satan, the prince of darkness. John first shows that this war has been raging since Genesis 3. A dragon pursues a woman. The woman represents the people of God while the dragon is Satan (12:1–6). She gives birth to a child who will rule, and she flees to a place of protection for a time. A second vision also includes the dragon, but this time Michael and his angels battle the dragon (12:7–12). He is the ancient serpent who is thrown down. On the earth, he pursues the woman, but she is given the wings of an eagle, and he goes off to make war on her children (12:13–17). The scene shifts to two beasts. The dragon enlists commanders to execute war on the woman's children (13). One beast comes from the sea and another from the earth. The dragon and the beasts are the unholy trinity. They make war on the saints and stamp their number and name on people. However, like in the other sections, the holy ones are protected. Chapter 14 propels readers to the heavenly Mount Zion, where the 144,000 stand with the Father and Lamb (14:1–6). These people have the names of the Lamb and the Father on their forehead, in contrast to the mark of the beast. They worship at the throne with the elders. Three angels are introduced, and then two harvests of the earth commence (14:7–20). There are only two groups: those rescued and those judged. Resist the beasts and follow the Lamb or suffer a winepress of fury.

Seven Bowls (15–16) / The seven bowls repeat the scene of the seals and trumpets, but do so in climactic fashion. John once again brings his readers to the end of history. However, the bowls are worse than anything readers have seen before. The cycle is preceded by a scene of worship, mirroring the song of Moses (15:1–8). It prepares readers for the bowls as Moses watched Egypt perish at the Red Sea. The bowls, like many of the judgments, echo the plagues inflicted on Egypt. The first four bowls strike the natural world (earth, sea, rivers, sun), while the last three strike the kingdom of the beast (16:2–21). On earth there are sores, the seas and rivers turn to blood, and people are scorched by the sun. The fifth bowl brings darkness to the beast's kingdom (16:10–11). The sixth bowl shows the enemies of God gathering for war, the battle of Armageddon (16:12–16). The enemies of God march toward their own destruction. The battle is over before it starts. The seventh bowl gives a final but repeated angle on the destruction of the earth as another earthquake cripples creation (16:17–21). The next chapter will zoom in and expand upon the fall of "Babylon the Great." That glorious day is coming, but not yet, so John tells his hearers to persevere and conquer.

Babylon Falls (17:1–19:10) / Two cities rage. Two female futures are at stake. John has painted the end of history in various ways; now he displays it as the destruction of a city and harlot in contrast to the bride, the New Jerusalem. Babylon is first introduced as an attractive, deceptive prostitute (17:1–6). The kings of the earth have slept with her. Her secrets are disclosed (17:7–14), and then her destiny is foretold (17:15–18). Her power comes from the beast, but the beast and kings will turn against this woman and consume her. Therefore, Babylon falls (18:1–8). She will be a desolate place, and they must flee from her so they don't share her fate. The responses to Babylon's destruction are both lamentation (18:9–19) and rejoicing (18:20–19:5). The kings, merchants, and seafarers lament because their wealth is gone. But the saints, apostles, and prophets rejoice. Now the Lamb and His bride are married (19:6–10). The harlot's clothing was spoiled, but the bride has fine linen, bright and pure.

Triumph (19:11–20:15) / Readers are now transported to another viewpoint of the battle. Rather than looking at the destruction of Babylon, John looks up and sees Christ's return. He is riding on a horse as the divine warrior. He judges the earth and conducts the only just war with a robe dipped in blood (19:11–21). He crushes those under His feet who have opposed Him, fire comes from His eyes, and a sword from His mouth. The birds of the air feast on the flesh of the kings of the earth after He has demolished them. The beast and the false prophet are thrown into the lake of fire. The victory is further described as the binding of Satan, who is thrown into a pit, and then Jesus' people reign with Him for a thousand years (20:1–10). After the battle is won comes the last judgment, where readers return to the throne (20:11–15). The book has now come full circle. It started in the throne room and ends in the throne room. But more is to come. Judgment clears the path for peace.

New Creation (21:1–22:5) / The final vision is of a new heaven and new earth. In the midst of them is the New Jerusalem. It begins with a wide-angle lens (21:1–8). The new creation is announced, the holy city is prepared as a bride. Babylon the harlot has been destroyed, and the bride of the Lamb is dressed for her husband. A voice announces that God will dwell with His people, and there will no longer be any sadness. This promise is only for conquerors. The faithless will be thrown into the fire that burns forever. Then readers see a more detailed description of the New Jerusalem (21:9–27). The city is on a high mountain, it shimmers, and has twelve gates and foundation stones. It is a perfect cube, resembling the holy of holies, and its measurement points to flawlessness. There is no sun or moon, because the glory of God is in its midst. Its gates are always open, and there is no darkness. The nations bring their glory and honor to the city like the wise men brought gifts to Jesus. However, it is not only a city, but a new

Eden (22:1–5). A river is in the middle of the city, the tree of life, and nothing will be cursed like after the fall. The river flows from the throne, giving life to all the inhabitants. The people in the city will see God forever, and His name will be on their foreheads. They are all priests to God. The Lamb has defeated the dragon.

Epilogue (22:6–21) / The epilogue matches the prologue (1:1–8). At numerous times in the narrative, John has heard God state that He is the beginning and the end, the first and the last, the One who was, who is, and who is to come, the Alpha and Omega. This vision of history comes from God Himself because He can see all. John has simply had the curtain lifted for him. John can trust these words are true because the triune God is trustworthy. God's angel has been sent to John to make these things known. Blessed are those who conquer and keep these words. Jesus will return soon, and He will repay those who do not follow His words. Curses and judgment await those who do not listen. The tree of life waits for those who are faithful. All who are thirsty are welcome to come and drink from the fountain of life. Jesus is coming soon. The time to decide is now.

ACKNOWLEDGMENTS

The writing of this book presented unique challenges. To think of images that matched sections of Scriptures was its own challenge. Then to design them in a visually appealing way added to the complexity. Finally, to summarize large sections of Scripture into readable paragraphs was like trying to put an extra-large turkey in a small oven.

The process was made more enjoyable as I worked with Anthony. We labored through our options, sometimes for hours, and I pressed toward faithfulness to the text while he pushed toward what would work graphically. We hope the product is something readers will benefit from.

Special thanks goes to Anthony and his detailed work on these designs. Thanks to many pastors and scholars who gave me feedback on initial outlines. Thanks to Connor Sterchi and Quinn Mosier for their editing help. Thanks to Drew Dyck and Moody, who believed in this project from the start.

STUDY THE BIBLE WITH PROFESSORS FROM MOODY BIBLE INSTITUTE

Study the Bible with a team of thirty Moody Bible Institute professors. This in-depth, user-friendly, one-volume commentary will help you better understand and apply God's Word to all of life. Additional study helps include maps, charts, bibliographies for further reading, and a subject and Scripture index.

978-0-8024-2867-7 | also available as an eBook

GET YOUR STUDENTS DIGGING DEEP INTO
THE TEXTBOOK THAT MATTERS MOST

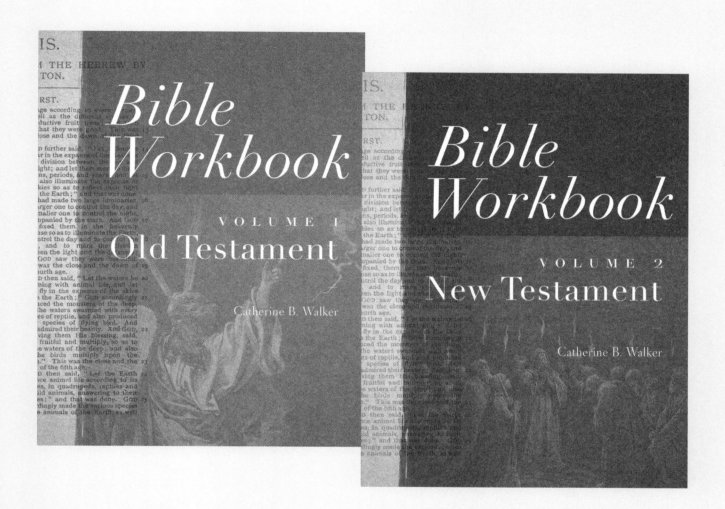

MOODY
Publishers®

From the Word to Life®

These Bible Workbooks are full of exercises, questions, and maps that ensure students have the fundamentals down before you teach. Each workbook contains thousands of fill-in-the-blank questions as well as diagrams and maps that students can interact with. The workbooks can be adapted for virtually any teaching setting (homeschool, Bible class, adult Sunday school).

Volume 1: 978-0-8024-0751-1
Volume 2: 978-1-57567-638-8

A rich treasury of Bible knowledge.

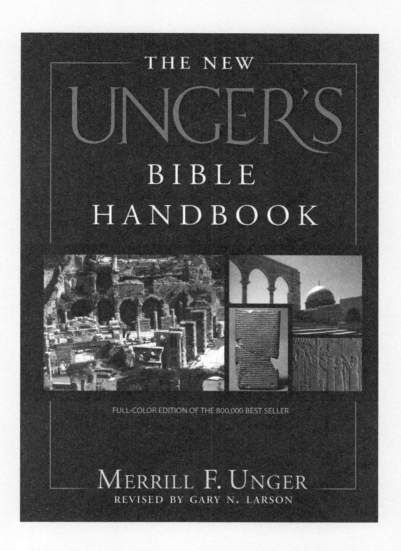

Seminary is an important step toward ministry— but only when you make the most of it.

Prepare for your calling and make the most of your theological training with *Succeeding at Seminary*. You'll learn how to select the right institution and weigh the pros and cons of online or in-person classes. You'll also receive tips for developing rapport with peers and professors and get insights for how to navigate a work, study, and family-life balance to help you survive the rigors of advanced theological learning.

978-0-8024-2632-1 | also available as eBook and audiobook